Anti GraVity

D0168009

Anti Gra^Vity

ALLEGEDLY HUMOROUS WRITING FROM *SCIENTIFIC AMERICAN*

Steve Mirsky

Foreword by John Rennie

THE LYONS PRESS
Guilford, Connecticut
An imprint of The Globe Pequot Press

To my parents, for being funny

To buy books in quantity for corporate use
or incentives, call **(800) 962–0973**
or e-mail **premiums@GlobePequot.com**.

Introduction, page ix; "An Axis to Grind," page 14; "Dropping One for Science," page 38; and "He Shoots, He Scars," page 115 copyright © Steve Mirsky. Reprinted by permission.

All other text copyright © 2007 *Scientific American, Inc.*

ALL RIGHTS RESERVED. No part of this book may be reproduced or transmitted in any form by any means, electronic or mechanical, including photocopying and recording, or by any information storage and retrieval system, except as may be expressly permitted in writing from the publisher. Requests for permission should be addressed to The Lyons Press, Attn: Rights and Permissions Department, P.O. Box 480, Guilford, CT 06437.

The Lyons Press is an imprint of The Globe Pequot Press.

10 9 8 7 6 5 4 3 2 1

Printed in the United States of America

Edited by David L. Green
Designed by Georgiana Goodwin

ISBN: 978-1-59921-115-2

Library of Congress Cataloging-in-Publication Data is available on file.

Foreword

Inside the walls of *Scientific American*'s laboratory offices in the Fortress of Sullenness at the North Pole, the editors toil endlessly at the grinding chore of making the world safe for science, and it leaves them little time for merriment or the perplexing affairs of mere mortals. Steve Mirsky is the exception. He rolls into our office bursting with good humor, and wrath at political outrages, and enthusiastic talk of baseball (which, I gather, is a sporting event of some kind). Frankly, it's unendurable to us, and so we asked him to direct his energies into a regular column, "Anti Gravity." To our amazement, Steve's column has become one of the magazine's most popular departments. Each month for more than a decade he has filed these entertaining, densely witty musings on science, nature, culture, and the human capacity for goofiness. In your hands, you hold the best of them. True, annoyed readers occasionally write to complain, "There is no place in *Scientific American* for this sort of silliness!" But I reply, "Of course there is, right there on page 96."

—John Rennie
Editor in Chief, *Scientific American*

CONTENTS

Introduction

Albert Einstein was a funny guy. Which is good, because if you're going to overturn an entire view of the universe, it helps to have a sense of humor. In fact, as you can read in these pages, Einstein is thought to have attempted to entertain his pet parrot with bad jokes. (What bad jokes would Einstein have told? Turn to page 192.)

The great physicist also had an almost yogilike outlook on the world—in the Berra sense. He reportedly once said, "If we knew what it was we were doing, it would not be called research." And as you'll also read in this volume, when asked for a simple explanation of relativity, Einstein said, "When you sit with a nice girl for two hours, it seems like two minutes. When you sit on a hot stove for two minutes, it seems like two hours. That's relativity."

Einstein thus proves that science and humor can walk hand in hand, although it's tough because, as Harvard historian of science Gerald Holton once put it, "In the sciences, we are now uniquely privileged to sit side by side with the giants on whose shoulders we stand." The point is that for more than a decade, I've been writing a column for *Scientific American* that is regarded, by some people, at some times, in some places, under the right conditions of temperature and pressure, to be funny.

This light column is called "Anti Gravity," in contrast to the *gravitas* of much of the rest of the magazine. Anti Gravity is the ice cream after an elegant and highly nutritious meal. It is sometimes referred to as a humor column, although I always defer to the reader's decision on that matter. Hence the subtitle of this collection of columns that span the years 1997 to 2006 is "allegedly humorous writing from *Scientific American*."

Much like *The Simpsons* was originally just some connective tissue on *The Tracey Ullman Show*, Anti Gravity grew from humble beginnings. The column's original purpose was to provide some pithy verbiage on which to hang a cartoon to gussy up the look of the news section. I had been a science writer for ten years when I was asked to come up with the pith. Why me? Probably because of a reputation for the odd wisecrack I sometimes buried in serious science reportage and because I type really fast. From its start as cartoon accompaniment, Anti Gravity has swelled, I mean beneficently grown, getting longer (from 450 words at first to its current 650 words per column), and metastasized, I mean been set free from its earlier confines in the news section to its own page at the back of each issue of *Scientific American*.

I have learned in the course of writing the hundred-all-odd columns that there are three kinds of humorous science stories. Some science stories are born funny, like the one about the guy who dresses up in a moose suit to study moose up close (page 38); some science stories are made funny, like the one about maggot therapy (page 19); and some science stories have funniness thrust upon them, like the one that recommends fictional characters for inclusion into actual scientific societies (page 153).

So, despite our designation of the stories in this book as being *allegedly* humorous, I wager that when you read about the two-headed toad of Hopkinton (page 1) or the reason that maps of MIT include a unit of length called the *smoot* (page 70) or what the great evolutionary biologist Ernst Mayr said when watching a film about endangered bird species of New Guinea (page 92) or the real reasons why UFO sightings have bottomed out (page 105) or the correlation between tick-borne diseases and golf scores (page 115), you will give in to the occasional snort, chortle, or guffaw. And as you read, always keep in mind Einstein's immortal words: "Science is a wonderful thing if one does not have to earn one's living at it."

CHAPTER 1

Wild and Wacky

HEADS UP

EXTRAORDINARY CLAIMS REQUIRE EXTRAORDINARY EVIDENCE, OR AT LEAST A SECOND LOOK

July 2002

The official Linnean designation for our species is *Homo sapiens*, which translates to "wise man." It's kind of an inside joke, as a quick scan of the front page of the newspaper whatever day that you read this will probably show. And if scientists have a tough time coming up with an accurate name for ourselves, it's no surprise that classification of organisms in general can be a dicey proposition.

Take, for instance, the strange creature found by a four-year-old girl in Hopkinton, Massachusetts, in a swimming pool in the middle of April 2002. As the local paper, the *MetroWest Daily News,* described the situation in a headline, "Girl Finds Two-Headed Toad in Hopkinton." The accompanying article offered a detailed description of the marvelous sideshow attraction: "The two toads are stacked on top of each other.... The toad on top is smaller and a lighter color. Its front legs have grown into the back of the larger frog, and it appears the bottom jaw may be connected to the larger toad's head."

Now, a brief rumination about the logistics summarized in this account may bring to mind fairly normal animal activity often found on the Discovery Channel, the Learning Channel and, for that matter, the Playboy Channel. On the other hand, the author of the short newspaper piece was none other than the renowned novelist and trustworthy journalist Norman Mailer. Or so it seemed, because it's easy to make mistakes when a first glance appears to uncover something really special.

Indeed, a second glance revealed that the byline actually read "Norman Miller," presumably a staff reporter at the paper, not Norman Mailer. And, as the *MetroWest Daily News* reported three days later, a second glance at the beast with two heads revealed it to be the more common beast with two backs, a pair of one-headed *Bufos* boffing. Or, as the follow-up story succinctly put it, "It was just a couple of horny toads." The mistake presumably was listed in the paper's Errata *and* Erotica sections. (Please do not read the above as a knock on Mr. Miller, as merely getting things wrong is one of the great traditions of American journalism, still practiced everywhere. For example, many people consider this section of *Scientific American* to be an error every month.)

The tale of two toads shows that amateur mistakes may be amusing. But if you're looking for something done really wrong, turn to professionals, who also have problems classifying some of the oddball organisms cobbled together by evolution. One of the most spectacular and well-known examples was a creature considered so weird that it received the genus name *Hallucigenia*. In the original interpretation of the fossil remains, *Hallucigenia's* tube of a body rested on multiple pairs of stiff quills, while a row of seven tentacles, replete with what seemed to be mouths at the ends, waved from its back. Later fossil finds, however, revealed a second set of the tentacles alongside the first. The creature suddenly made a lot more sense if you turned it upside down: the twin sets of flexible appendages were probably its legs, and the daggers originally thought to be legs most likely stuck up from its back, protecting it and keeping paleontologists from ever finding a fossil of two of these things clamped together in an experts-only exercise from the Cambrian *Kama Sutra*.

Yes, misclassification can be fun. Unfortunately, a bad identification can also be fatal: it's far safer to make a mistake with a **Hallucigenia** fossil than with a hallucinogenic mushroom. The journal *Internal Medicine* recently reported on a mushroom-related death and noted that "it may be that those who seek hallucinogenic mushrooms are less discerning and more prone to species misidentification than other foragers." Such fungi foragers, therefore, are advised to consult a knowledgeable companion before biting any buttons. For, as has been demonstrated innumerably, two heads are better than one.

WILD LIFE

OF BEERS, BEARS, FISH, AND ASSAULT WITH A DEADLY REPTILE

November 2004

Human beings have close encounters with other species on a daily basis. For example, in the past twenty-four hours I have shaken a large spider from a bath towel; taken care not to hit a frog with my car; carried a hitchhiking grasshopper on my bike; been leapt on by a big dog; been rubbed against by a small cat; fed upon a chicken; been fed upon by a mosquito. Such a day is fairly tame. But this past summer you couldn't swing a dead alligator without hitting a news story about wild interactions between *Homo sapiens* and other organisms.

Take the guy who swung the *live* alligator. Here's the beginning of the Associated Press account, out of Port Orange, Florida, in July 2004: "A man hit his girlfriend with a three-foot alligator and threw beer bottles at her during an argument in the couple's mobile home, authorities said." This relatively short sentence (which is also what a judge will probably give the gator swinger) is so evocative that further comment would only dull its luster.

A few weeks later a better use of beer was discovered by an innocent ursine in the Pacific Northwest. "A black bear," the Reuters coverage began, "was found passed out at a campground in Washington State recently after guzzling down three dozen cans of a local beer." (Animal alcohol abuse is not unknown. In 2002 elephants in India found some rice beer and went on a drunken rampage. Many birds have found that flying and fermented berries don't mix.) Our buzzed bear, who busted into coolers at Baker Lake Resort, northeast of Seattle, drank his dinner discriminatingly: after trying another brand, the bear limited his libations to Rainier Beer. And that brewer appreciated what the market would, well, you know. Rainier named the bear its unofficial spokesbeast and then literally named the bear, through a contest. The winning entry was Brewtus, although I was hoping for either Logy Bear or, of course, Booze Booze.

And it's no surprise that bears have taken to drink, for it seems that more people have taken to bears—to eat. But the bears have a secret weapon. The Centers for Disease Control and Prevention's *Morbidity and Mortality Weekly Report* noted in July that "during 1997–2001, a total of seventy-two cases of trichinellosis . . . were reported to CDC; the majority of these infections were associated with eating wild game, predominantly bear." The bears harbor the trichinella roundworm, which happily infects people who keep too low a fire on Smokey. It's not exactly a rampaging epidemic, with an average of about twelve cases a year. But even that number puts the lie to the old adage "Sometimes you get the bear [pronounced "bar" in old adages], sometimes the bear gets you." More accurately, "Sometimes you get the bear, sometimes the bear gets you, and every once in a while you get the bear, a high fever, chills, aches, diarrhea, and a visit to a parasitologist."

Meanwhile bears and people share a taste for salmon. So the first sentence of an August press release from the

American Chemical Society (ACS) was of interest both to us and to any literate bears: "Farm-raised salmon contain much higher levels of flame retardants than most wild salmon, and some wild Chinook have the highest levels of all, according to new research."

The release, discussing a report in the ACS journal *Environmental Science & Technology*, revealed that many salmon now come with the secret ingredient polybrominated diphenyl ethers (PBDE), "used widely as flame-retardant additives in electronics and furniture." A salmon industry press release countered with the headline "Salmon Flame Retardant Study Shows No New Data; Consumers Should Not Be Alarmed." Or five-alarmed. Anyway, is it still okay to regularly consume salmon with FDNY, I mean, PBDE? The two sides disagree, no surprise, so I offer this helpful salmon rule of thumb: if you can't cook it, don't eat it. Fin.

SHORT TAKES

ONLY A SCIENTIST WOULD BRAG, "I ONCE CAUGHT A FISH THIS SMALL . . ."

April 2006

In late January 2006, a Brobdingnagian battle erupted over a Lilliputian water dweller. Okay, the battle wasn't really all that huge. And we're not talking about the Benihana shrimp toss case, a lawsuit that started in January. That ballyhoo *was* big and concerned a chef who flung sizzling shrimp into the mouths of his patrons. Hey, it's not just dinner, it's a show. Anyway, one guy dodged the shrimp, hurt his neck, went into a general health decline and eventually died. His widow sued for $16 million, which is a lot of clams. (In February the jury let Benihana off the hook, finding the restaurant not at fault.)

No, the fight in question concerns competing claims by scientists over the smallest of fry: the world's tiniest fish, which also makes them the world's shortest vertebrates. A multiinstitutional research team reported that it had discovered adult fish just 7.9 millimeters long. The species, *Paedocypris progenetica,* is found in incredibly acidic peat wetlands in Indonesia. "Tiny backbone living in corrosive swamp" would ordinarily describe a member of the House ethics committee, but in this case it's a kind of carp.

The scientists published their finding in *Proceedings of the Royal Society B: Biological Sciences*, a journal title that takes up a little more than ten times the space on this page than would the creature cited as the previous record holder for world's smallest vertebrate. That beastie is the eight-millimeter-long dwarf goby. Henceforth and in comparison to be known as the moby goby.

A quick aside: what you definitely don't use to catch any of these petite pisces is a *Driloleirus americanus*, better known (to probably half a dozen people) as the giant Palouse earthworm. In February a graduate student at the University of Idaho became the first person in almost twenty years to see one. It's a white worm, as Ahab might have noted, that can reach a length of one meter. Which is puny compared with some Australian earthworms that can be three meters long. Fortunately, they're down under down under.

Back to our untall tale. The print had barely dried on the various newspaper stories touting the teeny titleholder (talk about small victories) when a petition for priority appeared—the University of Washington was quick to point out that their Theodore W. Pietsch had plumbed new depths, or heights, I'm not sure which, in lack of length in September. Publishing in the Ichthyological Society of Japan's journal, *Ichthyological Research*, Pietsch revealed that full-grown males of the species *Photocorynus spiniceps*, a kind of anglerfish collected in the Philippines, have come in as small as 6.2 millimeters. These boys are more than (or less than, I'm not sure which) normal males. Female *P. spiniceps* can measure a massive 46 millimeters long—males are so small because they marry way up, engaging in what is known as sexual parasitism.

In his journal article, Pietsch explains sexual parasitism with this 1938 quote from naturalist William Beebe: "To be driven by impelling odor headlong upon a mate so gigantic, in such immense and forbidding darkness, and willfully to eat a hole in her soft side, to feel the gradually increasing transfusion of her blood through one's veins, to lose everything that marked one as other than a worm, to become a brainless, senseless thing that was a fish—this is sheer fiction, beyond all belief unless we have seen the proof of it." And you thought the Sigourney Weaver movie where the hideous monster latches onto its victim was bizarre. *Alien,* not *Working Girl.*

The minuscule male has chosen a life basically as a sex organ: the major occupants of its body cavity are its testes.

The female carries on all the usual functions of life for both, and the sole job of the mindless, attached male is to breed. And you thought the Tom Hanks movie where the dim-witted guy gets the girl was unbelievable. *Forrest Gump*, not *Splash*. In that one, the dim-witted guy gets the fish.

WHEN GOOD HIPPOS GO BAD

January 2000

Imagine a sport-utility vehicle interested in mating. That frightening scenario roughly captures your typical hippopotamus in rut. Hippos are big and surprisingly fast, able to reach speeds of twenty-five miles per hour. Unfortunately, anything of that size and speed may do inadvertent damage when in pursuit of an amorous adventure. Thus did a tragic death recently befall one Jean Ducuing, the director of a zoo near Bordeaux. Ducuing was killed by a charging hippo that may have been seeking intimacy with, or dominance over, nearby farm equipment.

The sex life of the hippo is far stranger than this incident illustrates. For one thing, hippos in the wild not only have sex, they also host it. Back in 1994, researchers publishing in the *Canadian Journal of Zoology* announced the amazing finding of a species of leech, *Placobdelloides jaegerskioeldi*, for which hippos are a secret love nest. In the researchers' own words: "Evidence suggests that mating in *P. jaegerskioeldi* is restricted to the rectum of the hippopotamus."(Restricted being the operative word.)

The scientists based their conclusion on the examination of fifty-three dead hippos, probably because rectal exams on live hippos are currently discouraged by all major research university health insurance plans. The only place on or in the hippos where sexually mature leeches were accompanied by spermatophores, or packages of sperm, was the rectum. Proof once again that anything Hollywood comes up with in its *Alien* movies or assorted rip-offs pales in comparison to the bizarre variations of the life cycle that evolution has patiently produced here on earth.

Fortunately for your average hippo, the immense creature has notoriously bad eyesight, which may help it maintain a sanguine attitude toward the foul play going on at its other end. Those feeble peepers might be at least partially responsible for the fatal charge that did in Ducuing. A poor self-image may also be a factor. How else to explain the fact that Komir, the French zoo's seven-year-old, two-ton male, apparently thought he was seeing either a female hippo or a competitor when in fact he was myopically gazing at a new tractor, which he decided to chase.

A key discovery that the ensuing tragedy made possible was that electrified fences are not sufficient deterrents to an inflamed hippo. Ducuing just happened to be at the wrong place at the very worst possible time, an innocent bicycler who was riding near the tractor when the hippo went after it. The *International Herald Tribune* actually quoted a zoo spokesperson as saying, "It was a crime of passion." Another zoo employee went on record with, "Komir had always been jealous of that tractor." Taking a page from local townspeople's handling of Frankenstein's monster, zoo workers used pitchforks to drive the hippo back into its enclosure.

Ironically, Ducuing had enjoyed a long and amicable relationship with Komir. The zoo director had trained the animal and had been photographed trustingly putting his head inside the hippo's gargantuan open jaws. Two tons of motivated meat, however, outweighs the fellowship of old friends.

Scientific American's Carol Ezzell recently had her own near-hippo experience. Ezzell, we are quite happy to report, survived. On assignment in Zimbabwe, Ezzell was in a Land Rover about fifteen feet from a seemingly docile, elderly male hippo when, provoked by Ezzell's guide, the beast suddenly roared and ran straight toward her. "And he moved fast," she testifies. "He covered the distance in a flash." That hippo, however, allowed Ezzell to return to us by emulating the leeches that most likely infest him. He turned tail.

SUPPLY AND DEMAND

May 1999

Ah, spring, and the thrill of romance is in the air. Why, the very name of this month bespeaks a time of year when potential takes center stage. "May." The word is pregnant with possibility.

Also pregnant this spring have been three chimps at the Los Angeles Zoo, which have unwittingly contributed to research illustrating what may be a vas deferens between the chimp reproductive system and our own. You see, the three male chimps that showed any interest in sex had all undergone vasectomies. A forty-five-year-old male named Toto, who had always seemed diffident when it came to matters of the heart and thus avoided the unkindest cut, allegedly waggled his finger at reporters and implied, "I did not have sex with those chimps."

Four adult females have been put on birth-control pills as a result of the unplanned pregnancies. Paternity tests will seek to determine if it's Toto who should tuck in the *Pan troglodytes* toddlers, or if any of the vasectomized males escaped their postoperative fate. And some veterinary student concentrating in wildlife pathology should be jumping all over a thesis ultimately to bear the title "Failure Rate of Vasectomies among Chimps."

Oddly enough, none of this business (chimps are not monkeys, so let's not go there) had anything to do with a wire story that ran just five days later under the headline "Banana War Escalates." That skirmish turned out to be nothing but a half-billion-dollar trade impasse between the U.S. and Europe, the result of tariffs hindering free-market forces.

A paper in the February 7 issue of *Proceedings of the Royal Society: Biological Sciences* also examined the effects of market forces, but not on bananas. The study looked at mate choice, a favorite subject among evolutionary biologists, in terms of the haggling associated with a free market. (And you wonder why you should have gotten a prenup.) For zoo chimps, mate choice basically depends on cage assignment. Although that situation bears an eerie similarity to many office relationships, human mate choice tends to be more complex. The decision-making process is difficult to observe in most species, but the researchers took advantage of a valuable tool for observing courtship negotiation unique to humanity: personal ads.

Most of the researchers' conclusions were fairly straightforward. Female market value appears to be largely a function of fecundity, for which age, or more accurately youth, is an indicator. Male market value depends mostly on income and "risk of future pair-bond termination." In turn, these characteristics hugely influence the kinds of demands that men and women are willing to make of prospective partners.

Surprisingly, most men understood their place in the market. The researchers plotted the number of traits men sought in a potential mate, such as age, attractiveness and social skills, versus the males' own market values. The result is a reasonably straight line—the higher a guy's market value, the more demands he seems willing to make of his prospective mate—but only with the removal of a key demographic group: men between forty-five and forty-nine years old. These guys had a low market value thanks to the enhanced probability of "pair-bond termination" as a result of death (their choice of "sucking in my gut" as favorite exercise regimen probably hurt too). But they made demands more in keeping with those of men having three times the market value.

Men making the transition from being relatively young to becoming relatively old apparently sometimes do so kicking and screaming a bit. Perhaps they could learn from Toto, age forty-five, who never seemed to make any demands at all on his female chimp acquaintances and thereby escaped the scalpel. If this Toto suddenly found himself before any great and powerful wish-granting wizards, he could remain blissfully silent, having no need for brain, heart, or any other replacement body parts.

AN AXIS TO GRIND

September 1997

Any man will tell you that the mammalian penis is pretty special, but such commentary is usually worthless. Now comes independent confirmation from a female scientist that the penis is indeed one of evolution's exceptional accomplishments.

Diane Kelly, a postdoctoral associate at the College of Veterinary Medicine at Cornell University, has a long interest in how organisms solve life's engineering challenges. At Duke University, Kelly studied the relation between form and function in the mammalian penis, work that appears in the August 1997 issue of the *Journal of Morphology*.

As hydrostatic organs, penises have to fill with fluid to adopt a reproducible, typical shape with structural integrity. Kelly had seen passing comments in the literature describing the human and dog penises as having collagen fibers apparently running perpendicular to one another. To extend those findings, she turned to the nine-banded armadillo, or peba.

"They're not endangered," Kelly says of her study subject, "and they're easy to get." As easy as collecting them from the roads near Tallahassee, where their horny coverings are no match for Florida drivers. What pebas really have going for them, however, is bang for the buck. "Their penis is about one-third of their body length when it's erect," Kelly notes. "So you can work with this nice big piece of tissue."

Doing those tests, however, meant giving dead armadillos erections, no mean accomplishment. "All the tissue I used had already been separated from the animals," Kelly explains. "So what you end up with is a little sock, with one open end." Tie off the opening, inject some saline, and voilà.

On erection, two crimped layers of collagen fibers straighten. An inner layer of collagen forms rings around the long axis while the outer layer makes for parallel lines along the axis. Kelly's careful measurements of the fiber angles, the first in the literature, showed that the angle between them was exactly ninety degrees, or orthogonal. The mammalian penis is thus the only hydrostatic organ reinforced by collagen fibers in this way.

Now, other biological systems have orthogonal fiber arrays—for example, worm bodies. In worms, however, the entire crosshatched array runs diagonally to the long axis, not along it, as in the penis. "Worms can bend" thanks to the alignment of the array, Kelly says. "The whole idea behind the penis is that you don't want it to bend."

Kelly also did quick takes on other mammalian species to make sure that the fiber array was similarly oriented. "I used tissue that people gave me," she confides. "It was amazing. At meetings I started talking to people about what I was doing, and then people started giving me things."

The fiber orthogonality and relation to the long axis give the mammalian penis qualities that are more sophisticated than those of other vertebrate penises. Although very good at withstanding head-on forces, the erect mammalian penis does have an Achilles' heel. "If the bending force is very large," Kelly elaborates, "the side in compression will tend to fail. And the kind of failure you get is a very sharp kink, like when you take a soda straw and you push on both ends. It'll bend for a little while in a curve, but then one end of it just goes. In engineering terms, it's called local buckling. And local buckling is often considered a sort of catastrophic failure." To be sure.

The medical literature does mention cases of "penile fracture," which appear to be unfortunate instances of the above scenario. "Subjects aren't very forthcoming about how they did it. So it's kind of hard to get hard data on that," Kelly says. At least one known veterinary example involves a very unhappy rhinoceros, whose charging days are very likely over. Those poor souls learned that the laws of nature, unlike some of its products, are strictly unbendable.

GORILLA IN OUR MIDST

July 1998

History was made in April when Koko, the signing gorilla, took part in the first live Internet "chat" between humans and another species, on America Online. Koko responded to questions posed by AOL subscribers, sometimes in a fashion that required elaboration by her mentor, Francine "Penny" Patterson. Recently *Scientific American* uncovered sections of the transcript that were mysteriously excised from the official, published version. We print them in the interests of better interspecies communication and to fill a gaping two-column hole left in our news section as we go to press.

To appreciate the value of the "lost Koko transcripts," here first are sections of the actual AOL chat of April 27.

> AOL Member: Koko, are you going to have a baby in the future?
> Koko: Pink.
> AOL Member: I'd like to know what you'd like for your birthday.
> Koko: Birthday. Food and smokes.
> Dr. Patterson: You have to understand . . . Smoke is also the name of her kitten.
> AOL Member: Do you feel love from the humans who have raised you and cared for you?
> Dr. Patterson: She's reading a birthday card.
> Koko: Lips, apple give me.

The recovered transcript remnants provide more detail and insight into Koko's thinking.

> *Recovered section 2:*
> Koko: Yes, Smoke is a kitten. But when I said smokes, I meant smokes. Cigars. Cubans, in fact. I know a guy who knows a guy who brings them in from Toronto.
> Gourmandy: What do you eat?
> Koko: I'm a vegetarian.
> Pittyting: What about having a baby?
> Koko: Pink. Like I said. I'm being ironic of course,

poking fun at human gender stereotypes. I mean,
I'd like a girl.

Washoerules: What bothers you?

Koko: Grad students. I am not an animal.

Well, you know what I mean.

Recovered section 7:

AnnSully: Is signing hard to learn?

Koko: I continue to confuse "heuristic" with
"hermeneutic."

MCrawford: Can you read?

Koko: I find Woody Allen's early writings piquant.
Hemingway used little words to say big things. I've
dabbled in Chomsky but find him pedantic, and I
disagree with fundamental aspects of his theses.
Goodall raises some interesting issues.

HennyYman: Where does a big gorilla like you
sleep, anyway?

Koko: Wait for it . . . anywhere I want. Of course.

Recovered section 11:

Bigstick99: Do you do any sports?

Koko: I get some exercise. I enjoy jumping up and
down on luggage. I also enjoy throwing luggage.

NobelLore: Do you follow the current scientific scene?

Koko: Unless a finding is published in the major
journals, one is unlikely to find mention of it in popular
reportage. I therefore attempt to browse the primary
literature when possible. Thank God for the Internet,
eh? LOL.

Recovered section 14:

Host: What did you think of your chat experience?

Koko: Frankly, I found it a bit jejune. I avoid chat rooms. I usually log on only to retrieve e-mail and check my stocks.

Host: Thank you. By the way, what is your e-mail address?

Koko: I don't give that out.

Host. Anything else you'd like to say?

Koko: Lips loose ships sink.

Host: What's that?

Koko: Good night.

SEMPER FLY

June 1999

As the son of a former U.S. Marine sergeant, I got quite used, whilst a feckless youth, to the charming and affectionate sobriquet "maggot." (And the marine in question was my mom. What I was called by my dad, also a former marine, would turn the air blue.) An almost familial pride therefore came over me when I saw some recent glowing press for actual maggots, specifically, the teeming, squirming, wormy offspring of blowflies.

The larval lauding appeared as a letter, entitled "Maggots Are Useful in Treating Infected or Necrotic Wounds," in the March 20, 1999, *British Medical Journal.* The maggots' beneficent medical potential comes from the future flies' habit of chewing diseased and dead tissue while eschewing the healthy stuff. The letter noted that they might be put to especially good use against flesh-eating bacteria that have become resistant to conventional antibiotic treatment.

Many a patient might opt for salt in their wounds before maggots. An hour spent in the dusty stacks of journals at a nearby medical school library, however, revealed that maggots have a long and illustrious place, dating to quite recently, in the physician's treatment armamentarium.

The elegantly written "Maggot Therapy: The Surgical Metamorphosis" appeared in the journal *Plastic and Reconstructive Surgery* in 1983. Had they done nothing else, the authors, Edward A. Pechter and Ronald A. Sherman, earned everlasting esteem for calling the derivation of the word "blowfly" an "entomologic etymologic exercise." But they also explained that accounts of maggots' ability to debride a wound go back about five centuries. War is indeed hell, sometimes of the Hieronymus Bosch variety—most of the early observations of maggoty goodness seem to have been made at various battles, in which wounded soldiers became the unwitting objects of scientific discourse simply by lying there long enough to have flies lay eggs on or in them.

A Baltimore physician named William S. Baer did the first serious studies of maggots and wound therapy in the 1920s. His curiosity became aroused by the case of two World War I soldiers apparently saved from death by maggots that kept them, their broken legs and their abdominal wounds company on a battlefield for a week. In 1931 he reported successfully treating dozens of cases of osteomyelitis, a devastating bone infection, with maggots. The term "maggot therapy" was no bother to Baer, but others recognized it as a public-relations nightmare. A 1933 paper suggested "larval therapy," but even that made people's skin crawl. Nevertheless, maggots treated burns, abscesses, leg ulcers and gangrene through the 1940s before being discarded for the most part, a victim of people's prejudices against roiling masses of creepy, crawly insects dining on their necrotic flesh. Go figure.

And that's too bad. Especially since the creeping and crawling may actually be part of the therapy—some researchers think the constant movement of the little critters stimulates the growth of fresh, healthy tissue. Maggots may possibly even release their own special brand of antibacterial agents. If the thought of them happily munching away at raw infections wasn't so downright nauseating, they might be staples in medicine cabinets around the country. (Chances are, if you have them in your cabinet now, it's really time to clean out that cabinet.)

Shakespeare pointed out that "we fat ourselves for maggots." The worms will crawl in and the worms will crawl out eventually anyway. We may as well open our arms, and our open wounds, to them now. Perhaps the latest term designed to lessen the gag factor—"biosurgery"—will finally do the trick and give medicinal maggots their long overdue image makeover. Then again, probably not.

STRIFE AFTER DEATH

September 1999

Freud said that sometimes a cigar is just a cigar. By the same logic, sometimes a snake is just a snake. Which is good, because I've been thinking a lot about snakes lately. Unprovoked, such contemplation might make me consider analysis of a Freudian nature, but these thoughts have clear inspiration—namely, the *New England Journal of Medicine (NEJM)* and the U.S. House of Representatives.

NEJM recently carried a letter with the striking title, "Envenomations by Rattlesnakes Thought to Be Dead." The authors, Jeffrey R. Suchard and Frank LoVecchio of the Good Samaritan Regional Medical Center in Phoenix, described five cases of men—only men do dumb stuff like this, apparently—who got the surprise of their life from snakes that had just shuffled off their own mortal coils. Make no mistake, these snakes were as dead as Julius Caesar. "They retain some primitive reflex actions for a short while after being killed," Suchard explains.

"Patient 1 bludgeoned a rattlesnake on the head with wood," the authors write in *NEJM*. Evidently he was smacking the snake's head with his own head. Patient 1 was bitten on the finger when he picked up the dead snake.

"Patient 2 shot a rattlesnake, striking the head several times, and observed no movement for three minutes." Patient 2 lifted the snake, got a dose of venom in his finger and became the subject of observation himself, at the hospital.

"Patient 3 shot and then decapitated a rattlesnake." And then picked it up. Patient 3 was a thorough guy. Now he's a thorough guy whose friends call him Lefty. Actually, he didn't lose a whole hand, just a finger. When Patient 3 picked up the dead head, the venom-loaded fangs caused enough tissue damage to make amputation necessary.

"Patient 4 was envenomated on his left ring finger and right index finger by a decapitated rattlesnake head that had been motionless for five minutes." Patient 4 thus contributed to medical science by establishing a minimum waiting period for safely picking up a severed rattlesnake head: more than five minutes. Actually, "decapitated snake heads are dangerous for between twenty and sixty minutes after removal from the body of the snake," Suchard notes. "If that's not dead, I don't know what is."

"Patient 5 was envenomated on the left index finger by a rattlesnake he had presumed to be dead from multiple gunshot wounds, including one to the head." Patient 5 apparently never heard of Rasputin.

The authors note that alcohol may often impair a man's judgment enough to make snake-handling seem like a righteous idea and that "education to prevent snakebites should include warnings against handling recently killed snakes." In the interests of science education and public safety, *Scientific American* therefore warns: Don't handle recently killed snakes.

Rattlers, of course, are more than just snakes. They are symbols of wildness and power, qualities that inspired American colonists to put them on some of the first

American flags, along with the written advice "Don't Tread on Me." Of course, the U.S. long ago replaced the rattler with stars and stripes. But the spirit of the old symbol and motto still lurks behind the newer flag, like a rattler under a slab.

So it came as a shock when the House of Representatives overwhelmingly approved a Constitutional amendment outlawing "desecration" of the flag. (Congress failed to address whether desecration of the flag includes wrapping oneself in it.) Such legislation is counterproductive, treading as it does on the free-speech guarantees of the First Amendment. It is also unnecessary. A seemingly destroyed rattler is still dangerous; a country that tolerates the occasional destruction of its symbols, including images directly descended from the rattlesnake, is still powerful.

WHAT'S WRONG WITH THIS PICTURE?

FOR FOOTBALL FANS IN THE SUNSHINE STATE, IT'S SOMETIMES THE GAME OF THE NAME

October 2003

In this world, nothing is certain but death and taxonomy. Everyone is interested in death, but few of us outside of the order Strigiformes give a hoot about taxonomy. Nevertheless, people can have taxonomy—which *Merriam-Webster's* defines as the "orderly classification of plants and animals according to their presumed natural relationships"—thrust upon them. Just ask the mortified folks at the University of Florida.

Two of Florida's major products are the fruits of *Citrus sinensis* trees and football. The University of Florida's football team is called the Gators, in honor of *Alligator mississippiensis*. Although the name might lead you to assume that the Gators would be the football team at the University of Mississippi, the gridiron gladiators—sorry, I was channeling melodramatic sportswriter Grantland Rice (*Oryza sativa*) for a second there—at Ole Miss are in fact the Rebels, an appellation that pays tribute to the halcyon days of yesteryear when some *Homo sapiens* fought for the right to own other *Homo sapiens*. Go figure.

The Linnean alligator moniker presumably derives from the fact that American alligators can be found along the southern stretches of the Mississippi River. Despite the geographical misappropriation, since 1987 *Alligator mississippiensis* has been Florida's official state reptile. Buckle your alligator belt, because things are about to get even more confusing.

In late July the University of Florida football team released its media guide for the 2003 season. They mailed out some 13,000 copies of the guide, which school officials thought featured a large and aggressive-looking alligator on the cover. Except that, on closer inspection, the gator turned out to be a croc. Conspicuously unconsulted University of Florida crocodilian (both alligators and crocodiles are referred to as crocodilians—I told you it would be confusing) expert Kent Vliet told the *Palm Beach Post* that the photograph was probably of the Nile crocodile, *Crocodylus niloticus,* a nasty beast indeed. Differences in the snout shapes and the appearance of the big, pointy teeth are dead, and I do mean dead, giveaways.

The pictured critter was not even the elusive American crocodile, *Crocodylus acutus.* Best estimates put the number of *acutus* individuals in Florida at somewhere between 500 and 1,200, a figure apparently arrived at via the same tallying methodology used in Florida elections.

Now, to the untrained eye, mistaking a crocodile for an alligator seems like a trifle. But it's a major deal taxonomically. The two species are grouped together within the family Crocodylidae. To put the relationship in perspective, human beings are in the family Hominidae, which we share with chimpanzees, gorillas, and orangutans. Therefore, the Florida fumble is roughly the equivalent of using a photo of a group of gorillas to illustrate the faculty, who probably feel like monkeys' uncles over the entire affair.

Despite the preceding ribbing, I don't want to be accused of piling on. We all make mistakes, which is why pencils come with erasers—except for golf pencils, because lying in golf is not a mistake—and why this magazine has an erratum section. *Scientific American* recently corrected an April [2003] news story that contended that, in one study, cloned pigs had variable numbers of teeth. In fact, they had variable numbers of teats. The reporter can blame a poor phone connection for our own pigskin faux pas.

Besides, the Florida folks have probably become immune by now, the gator gaffe having no doubt prompted plenty of abuse from their fellow Southeastern Conference members. These schools include the universities of Arkansas (the Razorbacks, a fancy name for hogs, *Sus scrofa*), South Carolina (the Gamecocks, a belligerent kind of chicken, *Gallus domesticus*) and Alabama (the Crimson Tide, presumably a bloom of the algae species *Karenia brevis*). All told, I think I'd rather find myself in one of Florida's numerous gatored communities. See ya later.

LIFE SAVERS

A SMALL BOOK CONTAINS THE WIT AND WISDOM TO MAKE EVEN THE WORST SITUATIONS JUST AWFUL

February 2001

During my last trip to Florida, which took place during that lovely time of year when the recounts begin to bloom, I took a break from television coverage of electoral-college chaos and chanced on a documentary about the less violent world of alligator wrestlers. One grizzled veteran sagely said of his necessarily undefeated record, "There's no such thing as a *pretty* good alligator wrestler."

That quote came to mind shortly after a friend handed me a Christmas present: a thin Florida-orange-colored volume called *The Worst-Case Scenario Survival Handbook*, by Joshua Piven and David Borgenicht. Think helpful hints from Heloise, if Heloise were a U.S. Navy SEAL.

I was deeply touched by my friend's gift of instructions on how to cope with medical and other assorted emergencies and vowed never again to be a passenger in her car. The first item I turned to, at random, was entitled "How to Fend Off a Shark." A confirmed land mammal, I pishtoshed the whole business, as I'm sure not stupid enough to get myself into a position in which I'd need to fend off a shark. I figured the book was a waste of time but riffled further to land quickly at "How to Wrestle Free from an Alligator." Whoa, I thought, now this is information I *am* stupid enough to need.

For a New Yorker who doesn't work in the sewers (as such), I'm near alligators a lot. Once, while dreamily strolling through the Loxahatchee National Wildlife Refuge just south of ballot-bouncing West Palm Beach, I stepped within inches of a gator sunning on a levee edge. Yes, you can come dangerously close to a six-foot-long reptile without seeing it if you fully commit to mental vacuity. He exploded down the bank into the water, and I resolved to pay more expletive attention.

In 1996, researching an Everglades story, I waded through waist-deep, gator-gorged waters with a park ranger named Bob Hicks. As we wandered, Hicks shared the self-knowledge he gained when, backpacking through the 'glades, he put his submerged foot down on top of a slightly more deeply submerged gator. The major part of the insight concerned a discovery about the quality of his screams. "I now know what I sound like when I'm scared," Hicks recalled. "It's not a high-pitched *aaahhhhhhhh!!!* It's more of an *uuuhhhh, uuuhhhh, uuuhhhh.* It's like a Moe, Larry, Curly thing." (Oddly enough, I learned the same Stoogey self-truth the night I fell face-first down a flight of stairs in the dark.)

Anyway, the handbook's unassailable instructions for getting away from an alligator that takes more of an offensive attitude than Hicks's or mine did are fairly straightforward. They include, "If its jaws are closed on something you want to remove (for example, a limb), tap or punch it on the snout." The authors' counsel concludes with "Seek medical attention immediately."

Worst-Case Scenario, which I now rate as a fine addition to my library, covers a variety of such topics, often citing scientific facts. For example, in the section "How to Escape from Quicksand," the authors offer this grainy guideline: "The viscosity of quicksand increases with shearing—move slowly so the viscosity is as low as possible." In "How to Jump from a Bridge or Cliff into a River," they note the importance of going in feetfirst: "If your legs hit the bottom, they will break. If your head hits, your skull will break." And in "How to Perform a Tracheotomy," they advise not to waste time sterilizing whatever instruments you're lucky enough to have: "Infection is the least of your worries at this point."

Unfortunately, in addition to neglecting instructions on how to fall safely face first down a flight of stairs in the dark, the handbook fails to address such worstest-case scenarios as "How to Unhang a Chad," "How to Complete an Overseas Absentee Ballot," and "How to Revive Dick Cheney." Perhaps in volume two.

Author's note in 2007: Add to that list "How to Survive Quail Hunting with Dick Cheney."

ENTER THE DRAGON EXHIBIT

ONCE UPON A TIME THERE WAS A DRAGON AND A BEAUTIFUL PRINCESS, I MEAN ACTRESS, WHO FORGOT THAT LARGE CARNIVORES HAVE A BASIC INSTINCT

September 2001

Journalists often cite an old bromide: "Dog Bites Man" is not news, but, on the other hand, "Man Bites Dog" is news. And on the other foot, which is exactly where it happened, "Komodo Dragon Bites Newspaper Editor" is definitely news. Especially when the newspaper editor in question is the *San Francisco Chronicle*'s semi-celebrity executive editor Phil Bronstein, who was bitten while getting a special up-close-and-perilous tour of the Los Angeles Zoo's Komodo exhibit in early June, arranged for him by his full-celebrity wife, the beautiful actress Sharon Stone. The visit was Stone's idea of an early Father's Day celebration, which often includes dinner out.

Evidently, a zookeeper advised Bronstein to remove his white sneakers so they wouldn't be confused with the dragon's customary meal of white rat. This strategy clearly backfired. A letter to the *Chronicle* asked, "Whose bright idea was it to remove the white shoes from the white feet of a white man in the hopes of not confusing a nearsighted, simpleminded, ravenously hungry lizard?"

I take umbrage at this reader's umbrage, and I feel I am in a unique position to comment on this incident. That position is seated, in front of my computer, far away from any Komodos. For one thing, the Komodo dragon is not merely a lizard. It is "the world's largest living lizard—a ferocious carnivore—found on the steep-sloped island of Komodo in the Lesser Sunda chain of the Indonesian archipelago," according to the hilarious and completely accurate bit by the legendary radio comedians Bob and Ray.

For another thing, the dragon was no doubt well fed, which zoo animals tend to be. As for nearsightedness, Claudio Ciofi of the Zoological Society of London, writing in the March 1999 issue of *Scientific American* revealed that "monitors [the Komodo is a species of monitor lizard] can see objects as far away as 300 meters, so vision does play a role in hunting, especially as their eyes are better at picking up movement than at discerning stationary objects."

For my final rejoinder to the *Chronicle* reader, I note that Komodos are more single-minded than simpleminded—as an ambush-predator, the Komodo must be cunning and stealthy. And it should probably stay downwind of its prey, what with its amazing body funk. In a lecture, Walter Auffenberg, the world's foremost Komodo expert and author of *The Behavioral Ecology of the Komodo Monitor* (which, by the way, makes a terrific Father's Day present), remembered the first dragon he met on Komodo: "God, he stank. Oh my goodness. God, he was smelly. I called him Stinky. I went back and told the family that I met Stinky." Auffenberg later learned that Stinky was a "psychotic animal that had probably killed two people on Komodo prior to our visit." Ahhh, good times.

Anyway, my interest in Komodos was born while working with Ciofi on his article. And even though I learned that the dragons' saliva harbors numerous species of septic bacteria that can kill even if the bite itself doesn't, I was still dumb enough to get next to a Komodo at the National Zoo in Washington, D.C. If you look very closely at the Ciofi story's photo credits, you'll see that I snapped the dragon. (By the way, *my* visit to the zoo's dragon enclosure was arranged for me by my beautiful actress wife, uh, *Morgan Fairchild*. Yeah, that's the ticket.)

Back in the glamorous world of celebrity maulings, Bronstein underwent surgery to reattach a few tendons, and both his foot and sense of humor seem intact. He told his own paper, "That's how it goes when a movie star and a dragon are involved." Meanwhile Stone's view of the foot-and-mouth business was more Grimm: "Very few women get to see their knight wrestle the dragon. And I think he's kind of fabulous. And kind of hot." With the raging infection that usually follows a Komodo bite, perhaps that heat was just a fever—the two subsequently divorced.

REQUIEM FOR A HEAVYWEIGHT

A SLOW AND STEADY—AND EXCEPTIONALLY LENGTHY—LIFE

September 2006

Four score and seven years and four score and nine more years ago, a tortoise hatched in the Galápagos. She spent the past half a century known as Harriet. For more than a century before that, she was called Harry. Before that she almost was called dinner, but fate had other plans. Her heart, which began beating when Abraham Lincoln was barely out of his teens, finally stopped on June 23.

Her fame came from her longevity and from her celebrity friends. She spent her last years at the Australia Zoo in Queensland, run by Terri and the late Steve "the Crocodile Hunter" Irwin. And she was most likely rescued from the soup tureen that she strongly resembled by Charles Darwin. Yes, that Charles Darwin, born the same day as Lincoln.

"I find her walk through time to be extraordinary," says Scott Thomson, a paleontologist and taxonomist at the University of Canberra in Australia, whose analysis of Harriet's DNA helped to show that her life began in 1830, give or take a couple years. Most of Harriet's history was hidden when Thomson started snooping around in the early 1990s as part of an effort aimed at determining the subspecies of all Galápagos tortoises in Australia. When that project started, Thomson knew that Harriet had come to the Australia Zoo (then known as the Queensland Reptile Park) in 1987. As Thomson, Irwin and Irwin wrote in a 1998 article in the journal *Reptilia*, in 1952 Harriet began living at a place called Fleay's Fauna Sanctuary. There she was finally recognized to have been a female all along. The mix-up is understandable, because determining the sex of a giant tortoise is problematic. For one thing, turning over a 330-pound, shelled reptile is no small feat. (Small feet are no giveaway either.) Internal genitalia make the exercise largely pointless anyway.

Pre-Fleay, she was at the Brisbane Botanical Gardens, living as Harry, named after the curator, one Harry Oakmann.

(Some of the gardens' trees may also have been named for him.) And records showed that Harry/Harriet was there at least as far back as 1870. A break in the case came in 1994, when an Australian newspaper ran a story about another giant tortoise, called Lonesome George because of his status as the last member of his subspecies. The article prompted a newspaper letter from a retired historian who remembered seeing tortoises, including Harry/Harriet, in Brisbane back in the 1920s—and being told that they had been brought by a Captain Wickham from England.

Wickham was first lieutenant to Captain FitzRoy on the *Beagle*, the ship that carried the young naturalist Charles Darwin from 1831 to 1836. And Darwin was the most likely person to have collected Harriet.

Some reports pour cold water on the Darwin connection, because Thomson's DNA analysis showed that Harriet was a member of a subspecies native to Santa Cruz Island which Darwin never visited. But Darwin did collect tortoises on Santa Maria Island—even though the Marian subspecies had been driven to extinction by hungry inmates of the local prison, unfamiliar with the concept of sustainable development. The prison thus restocked its cupboards with tortoises captured on other Galápagos islands. Strong circumstantial evidence therefore puts the juvenile Harriet on Santa Cruz, where she gets incarcerated by cons, carried to Santa Maria and plucked from the pot by Darwin.

After that near-broth experience, the next 170 years were a cakewalk. But all good things, even those long postponed, must finally end. "It's very sad that she died," Thomson says. "I knew Harriet for over twenty years, and she came to mean a lot to me. She loved people more than any other tortoise I have ever met." And the *Times* of London, not ordinarily given to eulogizing tortoises, paid this tribute: "Harriet created less trouble in the world than any other living creature, four-legged or biped." She certainly caused less trouble for some people than that biped Darwin.

FOR THE BIRDS

HAWKING INTERESTING AVIANS IN THE URBAN ENVIRONMENT

July 2006

New York City is lousy with birds, and I mean that in a good way: I once counted twenty species in an hour in my backyard in the Bronx, with rufous-sided towhees and American redstarts making cameo appearances beside the usual mourning doves and sparrows. The city is also clearly a human-dominated landscape. So the American Museum of Natural History was a good choice to host a late April conference called "Conserving Birds in Human-Dominated Landscapes." I went because in the Alfred Hitchcock movie *The Birds,* I rooted for the crows. (I also sided with the giant insects in *Starship Troopers.* Although I did back the humans in the *Matrix* movies. Well, in the first one.)

One of the speakers at the conference was Andrew Balmford of the University of Cambridge. In 2003 Balmford was named one of the "Scientific American 50," a celebration of research leaders "who have contributed to the advancement of technology in the realms of science, engineering, commerce and public policy." Balmford was recognized for his work on the economics of habitat preservation. So naturally we talked about inebriation and Pokémon.

Balmford discussed some birds' abilities to prosper among humans. The wood pigeon, for example, seems to have thrived in England by leaving its traditional woodland environment for the fields, where it has switched from a mostly fruit diet to crops (which some farmers aren't cooing about). Some wood pigeons have even taken up residence in towns and cities, where they hang out near bars—because of the great opportunities such establishments afford for the distribution of food directly onto the sidewalk. If you get my drift. (When I mentioned this pigeon propensity to a friend, he asked, "Food that was thrown out?" To which I responded, "Well, not *out*.")

As for the fictional cartoon creatures, in 2002 Balmford and his colleagues published a short report in the journal *Science* called "Why Conservationists Should Heed Pokémon." His two sons had an interest in the local flora and fauna, whereas most of their friends were much more engaged by Pokémon characters. "And it turns out there is actually a field guide to Pokémon creatures in which you can learn all their different names and all their different attributes," Balmford says, "just like you would about birds of the eastern U.S." Balmford decided to find out which group of creatures most kids knew better: a sampling of the real animals and plants in their area or the Pokémon organisms. You know where this is going.

According to the *Science* paper, "For wildlife, mean identification success rose from 32 percent at age four to 53 percent at age eight and then fell slightly; for Pokémon, it rose from 7 percent at age four to 78 percent by age eight, with children ages eight and above typically identifying Pokémon 'species' substantially better than organisms such as oak trees or badgers." Says Balmford of that finding, "We obviously felt that was rather sad. Sad and rather worrying, but it also maybe can give us some food for thought about how we market natural history to kids to capture their imaginations."

Such inspiration should be possible, because birds really are incredibly charismatic. Here's one possible sample pitch for the get-kids-into-birds campaign: Now, I admit to almost complete ignorance about Pokémon characters, which I would imagine do incredible things, like shoot fire out of their blowholes or eat rocks or design a high-mileage, low-emission SUV or other magical things. But birds can do some pretty amazing things themselves. Some can outrun thoroughbred horses, others can pluck fish out of raging rivers with their feet, a few can see a rabbit a mile away. And of course, the big one—they fly! In fact, numerous residents of Metropolis, when getting their first glimpse of no less a personage than Superman, shouted, "Look, up in the sky! It's a bird!"

DROPPING ONE FOR SCIENCE

February 1997

OK, let's cut right to the chase. The reason the guy gets into the moose suit is because he couldn't throw the dung far enough.

Well, maybe we should back up. For the past two decades, conservation biologist Joel Berger of the University of Nevada at Reno has studied the behavioral, ecological, and reproductive biology of mammals. For the past two years, he has focused on the relationship between predator and prey in the greater Yellowstone National Park area and in south-central Alaska. "Our research is concerned with what happens to prey in systems where large carnivores are absent," he told a group of reporters last November at New York City's Central Park Zoo, part of the Wildlife Conservation Society, which funds his current research. "This is important, because in most of the world, systems are going to be losing large carnivores, rather than gaining them."

Both study sites contain a favorite food of grizzly bears and wolves, namely, moose. (See, we're getting there.) Grizzlies and wolves, however, are much more common in Alaska than around Yellowstone. This discrepancy has some easily quantifiable effects. A century ago moose were rare around Jackson Hole, in the Yellowstone area; they thrive now. More than 90 percent of moose calves survive every year at Jackson Hole, whereas only about 35 percent do in Alaska. From the moose perspective in Yellowstone, times are good.

One thing Berger wants to know, therefore, is how deeply those good times affect behavior: might prey animals begin to forget sensory cues warning of danger? So he and his colleagues played recordings of predator calls to moose at the different sites. "In Wyoming, moose failed to respond to wolf calls," Berger says. "In Alaska, they are sensitive and reduce the time they spend feeding by about half." Another cue should be odor. To test moose reaction to smell, Berger uses two potent sources of predator scent: urine and dung.

Getting the dung is one thing, the basic strategy being to wander around and pick up grizzly and wolf scat. Depositing it close enough to the moose to observe systematically their reactions to the smell is a messier issue. You cannot simply walk up to a moose. They're big, they're dangerous, they're scared—think of the 1996 New York Jets. Apparently, Berger did. "I had played some ball in college," the forty-four-year-old Berger says, "and could still throw reasonably accurately." Those throws weren't far enough, however. "We tried slingshots," he continues, "but they don't work so well. You can only get a small amount through. We tried longer and longer slingshots, but then you get sound effects." And hurling urine remained a problem as well.

Declining the opportunity to experiment with catapults or, for that matter, moosapults or scatapults, Berger was left with an old strategy: if you can't beat 'em, join 'em. A designer from the *Star Wars* movies created the moose suit, which looks like something two people would get into for a Halloween party, but which looks like a moose to other moose, who don't see all that well. The idea is to stroll up to a real moose, drop off some scat, avoid getting mounted and saunter away. Preliminary tests of the suit showed that moose seemed unperturbed.

Bison, though, "ran like hell," according to Berger, which may mean that they see better or simply don't like moose. If everything has gone well, Berger and his wife and colleague, Carol Cunningham, will have spent much of this winter in the suit. (At the same time—she's in back.) Before leaving the zoo to return west, Berger was asked if he had any concerns about safety. He answered simply, "Lots."

VISITING ROYALTY

MONARCHS FROM MAINE AND MICHIGAN WAIT OUT THE WINTER ON A MEXICAN MOUNTAINSIDE

April 2004

There are many compelling vistas for the traveler heading west of Mexico City on Route 15. The extinct Nevado de Toluca volcano, for example, dominates the scene to the left. Within its now quiet caldera lie two lakes, which, at an altitude of more than 15,000 feet, are among the highest places in the world where people scuba dive. The volcano's lakes thus offer the opportunity to get altitude sickness and the bends at the same time.

Then there are the views to the right as Route 15 turns from a busy highway into a twisting, two-lane mountain road. Pondering the sheer drops from the switchbacks my bus is negotiating can be the cause of—or cure for, depending on one's particular physiology—the gastrointestinal problems this part of the world is famous for inadvertently inflicting on gringos like me.

The bus, carrying a mostly gringo group of junketing journalists on this late January day, is wending its way to the small mountain town of Angangueo, where we'll spend the night. The next morning we will continue on to Sierra Chincua. This reserve is one of perhaps 20 pockets of fir forest, totaling only about 65 acres, that have just the right balance of temperature—usually—and humidity to be attractive to the quarter of a billion monarch butterflies (*Danaus plexippus*) that fly to them from eastern Canada and the U.S. to spend the winter. The phenomenon is not unlike that other great natural migration, spring break. The butterflies, however, will leave as mature adults.

After five hours, we at last pull up to our inn, along the steep, narrow main drag of Angangueo at dusk. How steep is the drag? The sidewalks have stairs built into them. After dinner, we see a map of the region in which landowners get paid to not cut down the fir trees that protect the butterflies through the winter. (The situation is streamlined in the U.S., where we pay landowners not to grow crops in the first place.)

In the morning we get back on the bus and climb further into the mountains until we reach the entrance to Sierra Chincua, where it's not just unusually cold, it's white—the night brought snow, and more soon begins to fall. Butterflies actually flying are probably off the menu for today. We're now at an elevation of more than 10,000 feet, with about two miles of hilly terrain to traverse to get to the fir trees we expect to be shielding the butterflies from the weather. Most of our party hops onto horses to make the trip. Claudio Angelo, a Brazilian science journalist, and I decide to hoof it ourselves, figuring that the walk will warm us up. "Besides," he says, "I don't feel like sitting on a wet, sweaty, smelly horse." A few minutes of hiking up hilly, muddy terrain at altitude, however, makes me paraphrase the famous words of Nietzsche: That which doesn't kill you makes you smell strong. In fact, the horses are giving us dirty looks.

Finally, we reach the butterflies, which have been grounded by the weather. Two days before, I had strolled down the Calle de los Muertos (Avenue of the Dead) amid the pyramids at Teotihuacán. The trail at Sierra Cinchua looks like a road of death as well, littered with thousands of butterflies. Turns out it's merely the calle de los frios. Walking carefully among the cold monarchs, we see that—as was said of Monty Python's parrot—they're not dead, they're resting, protected by a natural antifreeze compound in their bodies.

I pick one up and warm it with my breath. Suddenly the wings open. Startled, I nearly stagger backward, but I know that any random footsteps could probably take out about 20 other monarchs. So I stand my ground and place the almost fluttering butterfly on a tree trunk. This one may be lucky enough to begin the trip back to the U.S. in the spring. Here's hoping it and its northbound progeny avoid the windshields of southbound college students.

NOW YOU SEE IT, NOW YOU DON'T

May 1998

Picture the Beatles in a boat on a river, with or without tangerine trees and marmalade skies. They're chasing another boat. Assume that Rolling Stone Keith Richards is piloting that other boat, so its path is highly erratic. The Beatles pursue, turning their boat while continuously closing the distance to their prey. Hey, it could happen.

Switching from Beatles to beetles reveals, however, that pursuit of prey in one corner of the insect world turns out to be far less smooth. As was first reported more than seventy years ago, hungry tiger beetles, which have compound if not kaleidoscope eyes, run as fast as they can toward a prospective live meal but then come to a screeching stop. During this time-out, the beetles reorient toward their sidestepping targets. After zeroing in again, they resume running as fast as they can. They may have to do this three or four times before catching their prey or giving up.

Cole Gilbert, an entomologist at Cornell University, has seen this halting hunting technique in the woods near his lab. Finding the beetles' mystery tour toward their prey vexing, Gilbert decided to observe the stuttering stalkers under controlled conditions.

Gilbert set individuals loose after fruit flies, pursuits that he filmed and analyzed down to the millisecond. Without any direct studies of the beetles' eyes or brains, Gilbert came to a few conclusions about their sensory system and their behavior, which he published in the *Journal of Comparative Physiology*. Based on the angular movements of the prey, the angles between neighboring ommatidia (the units of the beetles' compound eyes) and the duration of beetle breaks, Gilbert thinks beetles, which don't see all that clearly to begin with, actually out-run their visual systems.

"Think of Elmer Fudd when he's scanning with binoculars," Gilbert explains. "So Elmer is looking for the wabbit." (Gilbert actually said "wabbit.") "And he's going pretty fast, and then there's a little blip, a slight change in light intensity in those fields. He goes past it, and then he backs up and there's Bugs chewing his carrot." The faster he pans, the smaller Bugs's blip gets. Eventually, Elmer pans so fast that too few bunny photons fall on Elmer's photoreceptors. Bugs is, in effect, invisible to Elmer's sensors. Result: no wabbit stew.

Gilbert contends that, in a similar way, the movement of the prey, combined with the beetle's own speed, results in too few prey photons making it to the beetle's photoreceptor. In effect, the beetle goes blind until it can stop and reduce the relative velocity of the prey to the point where it registers again on beetle radar.

The consideration of such biological tracking systems might help optimize devices such as the Mars Rover, Gilbert believes. "You want to move quickly to explore a large area, but if you move too fast for the optical sensors to gather enough information to form an image, the exploration is fruitless. Through knowledge of biological tracking systems, we can learn how nature has coped with this trade-off. It might allow for strategies that engineers wouldn't necessarily think of."

The intermittent sensing of the beetles might be a leaner and more efficient system than one with enough circuitry to incorporate a constant feedback of information and response. Which means that it sometimes makes sense to take the long and winding road.

SIX-LEGGED CINEMA

THE BIG SCREEN HAS BEEN BESET BY BUGS SINCE THE BEGINNING

October 2004

They're baaaack.

I'm not referring to some horror movie monster, although that's what the line most likely conjures up in the imagination. I'm talking about May R. Berenbaum and Richard J. Leskosky, who have once again teamed up to write a scholarly piece sure to interest all fans of the science in science fiction.

Berenbaum is head of the entomology department at the University of Illinois, and Leskosky is assistant director of the Unit for Cinema Studies at the same institution. Over a decade ago, the married couple wrote "Life History Strategies and Population Biology in Science Fiction Films," an article showing that the overwhelming majority of invading aliens in sci-fi movies are doomed by their own biology.

[See "Nothing Personal, You're Just Not My Type," Science and the Citizen, *Scientific American*, February 1995.] Most sci-fi flicks feature more or less human-size creatures that show up and expect to be running things in no time. True, that approach actually worked for Arnold Schwarzenegger, but in real life, successful colonizers tend to be small organisms that produce huge numbers of offspring—for example, insects and studio executives.

More recently, Berenbaum and Leskosky wrote a piece for movie bugs on movie bugs: "Insects in Movies" appears in the new volume *Encyclopedia of Insects*. The entry reveals that moviemakers sometimes step all over bugs. "What constitutes an insect in cinema is not necessarily consistent with scientific standards," Berenbaum and Leskosky write. "In the taxonomy of cinema, any jointed-legged, segmented organism with an exoskeleton is likely to be classified as an insect, irrespective of how many legs or how few antennae it possesses." No less a polymath than Sherlock Holmes seemingly can't count. He incorrectly refers to a spider as an insect in 1944's *Sherlock Holmes and the Spider Woman*, which is about as elementary an entomological error as you can make. (And, yes, bugs should not technically be used as a synonym for insects, but we're taking etymological license.)

"Insect pheromones figure prominently in insect fear films," Berenbaum and Leskosky note, although in the 1978 movie *The Bees*, the characters call the chemical communication compounds "pherones." Lose the "er" too, and the insects could just call each other.

Berenbaum and Leskosky point out that although pheromones exist throughout nature, including in humans, they are rarely encountered in film in organisms other than insects. But 1977's *Empire of the Ants* acknowledges the human susceptibility to pheromonic influence: "Giant ants," Berenbaum and Leskosky explain, "use pheromones to enslave the local human population and to compel the humans to operate a sugar factory for them." In Florida, this same phenomenon is called agribusiness.

And let's talk about humongous ants. "A recurring conceit in insect films is the violation of the constraint imposed by the ratio of surface area to volume," write the arthropod aficionados. As body size increases, the ratio of surface area to volume decreases. Insects get their oxygen by taking in air through openings on their body surface, and if they got big enough the demands of all that volume on the relatively small surface would suffocate them. And when they molted, losing their chitinous corset, they would literally sag to death. Gregor Samsa did not awake one morning to find that he had been turned into a gigantic insect.

Obstinate insects have even played a fundamental role in movie history, inspiring one of the earliest efforts in stop-action animation, the 1910 short film *Battle of the Stag Beetles*. Entomologist Wladyslaw Starewicz first tried filming stag beetles in action, but like many temperamental actors, they objected to the hot lights and refused to perform. "Accordingly," Berenbaum and Leskosky write, "[Starewicz] dismembered the beetles and wired their appendages back onto their carcasses, painstakingly repositioning them for sequential shots." Using that same technique, just think of the performances you could get out of Matthew McConaughey.

FEATHERS, FLIGHT, AND FAITH

March 1999

The whole town has just pitched in to save Jimmy Stewart's hide at the end of *It's a Wonderful Life*, and I'm watching and thinking, *not good enough*. Yeah, they may have covered the eight large that Uncle Billy lost, but what about fines and penalties?

I'm definitely in a funk. It's early winter 1999, and the Yankees aren't scheduled to beat up on the Red Sox again until May 18, and if all this impeachment nonsense hasn't slithered back under the rock it crawled out from by the time you're actually reading this in late February or March, my depression is going to be deep enough to perhaps warrant pharmaceutical intervention. All of which leads, inevitably of course, to Emily Dickinson.

The Belle of Amherst (that's Dickinson, for any readers who have been working on that chemistry or physics doctorate since George Bush the Elder was president) had the immortal insight once that "hope is the thing with feathers." Now comes a study that shows that while hope may have feathers, feathers had little hope, almost from their inception. Soon after evolution came up with the fantastic invention of the feather, it also cobbled together those annoying little bird banes, feather mites.

In *Nature*, researchers from the University of Portsmouth in England report the discovery of what certainly appear to be the fossilized eggs of mites sticking to a 120-million-year-old fossil feather. The feather was found in Brazil and eventually wound up at the National Science Museum of Japan. (I would bet that it flew there, showing that nature may not be malicious, but it is certainly ironic.) Between sixty-eight and seventy-five microns across, these attached tiny spheres—the feather had over 100—are the wrong shape and size to be the pollen grains or spores common to the same deposit in which the feather was found. Instead they closely resemble the eggs of parasitic mites that infest birds today. And they are stuck to the feather, which may not be a smoking gun, but hey, they've been on it for 120 million years. So it would seem that feathers, a supreme evolutionary achievement, were fouled from nearly the start.

My depression grows. Clearly, nature has decreed that any good thing be accompanied by its drawbacks—a conservation law, but of misery. And yet I find a ray of—dare I say it?—hope. This glimmer of possibility exists in a recent *Proceedings of the Royal Society of London* article. Researchers from Switzerland and Madagascar discovered a genus of mayflies that has renounced the potential inherent in its name and evolved stunted, ineffectual wings—it most definitely may *not* fly. That might seem like a bad thing, but wait.

This genus, *Cheirogenesia*, apparently gave up flight because the waterways in its Madagascar home are notoriously lacking in predatory fish. Other mayflies need to propel themselves from the water's surface to escape a fish-bait fate. The unthreatened *Cheirogenesia*, however, adapted and adopted a less flighty lifestyle, content merely to skim the water's surface. Its incredibly hopeful response to such a sanguine situation also had a lower cost of living; it was able to shift from expensive lipids to cheaper carbo-hydrates as its form of fuel storage. Being stuck at sea level, it could also devote more of its energy supplies to reproduc-tion than can its airborne mayfly relatives.

Like some insect version of the Amish, the *Cheirogenesia* rejected new-fangled technology and carved out a nice little niche indeed. Now, if predatory fish move into the neighbor-hood, these maynotflies are cooked. But right now times are good. My lifted spirits tell me that Ms. Dickinson can keep the feathers. Hope, in fact, is the thing with stubby wings.

THE TRIALS OF LIFE

BECAUSE ETERNAL VIGILANCE IS THE PRICE OF LIBERTY, WE HAVE TO TALK ABOUT INTELLIGENT DESIGN AGAIN. SORRY

December 2005

Let's review. First there was the oxymoronic, and just plain moronic, creation science, which says that biblical creation, not evolution, accounts for all life on earth. Creation science begat the more subtle intelligent design (ID), which holds that life is too complex to have evolved naturally—an intelligent designer (identity a secret, but it rhymes with Todd) must have done it, producing wonders of nature like the flagellum, that whippy tail some bacteria have, and both Angelina Jolie *and* Jennifer Aniston.

On September 13, 2005, the *New York Times* ran an article that discussed how the documentary *March of the Penguins* was a big hit among some groups because of the lessons it imparted. A reviewer in *World Magazine* thought that the fact that any fragile penguin egg survived the Antarctic climate made a "strong case for intelligent design." Conservative commentator Michael Medved thought the movie "passionately affirms traditional norms like monogamy, sacrifice, and child rearing."

Coincidentally, I had seen the movie just a few days before. On a blisteringly hot day in South Florida, I intelligently designed my afternoon to be in an air-conditioned theater watching penguins. So perhaps I can be of some help.

Penguins are not people, despite their natty appearance and upright ambulation. Their traditional norms include waddling around naked and regurgitating the kids' lunch. But it would be as absurd to castigate them for those activities as it is to congratulate them for their monogamy. Besides, the movie clearly notes that the penguins are *seasonally* monogamous—like other movie stars usually reviled by moralists, the penguins take a different mate each year. And there are problems with them as evidence of intelligent design. While caring for the egg, the penguins balance it on their feet against their warm bodies; if the egg slips to the ground for even a few seconds, it freezes and cracks open. A truly intelligent design might have included internal development, or thicker eggshells, or Miami. Finally, penguin parents take turns walking seventy miles to the sea for takeout meals. The *birds* have to *walk*.

From tribulations to trials. On September 26, I sat in a federal courtroom in Harrisburg, Pennsylvania, where a lawyer said for almost certainly the first time ever, "Can we have the bacterial flagellum, please?" This groundbreaking moment in legal history came on day one of the trial that will determine if the Dover, Pennsylvania, school board violated the First Amendment by introducing religion in a public school when it required the inclusion of an antievolution, pro-ID advisory in ninth-grade biology classes.

Dubbed "Scopes II" by some, the case is really "Scopes III." The 1987 U.S. Supreme Court case *Edwards v. Aguillard*, which barred creation science from public school science classrooms, was often dubbed "Scopes II." And you can't have two Scopes II's, at least not until the forces of irrationality begin futzing with the math curriculum too.

Members of the Dover school board who want ID taught are free to consult the opening paragraph for an explanation of ID. The curriculum chair, ID proponent William Buckingham, could have used some crib notes when he was asked in a deposition last January, "Do you have an understanding in very simple terms of what 'intelligent design' stands for? What does it teach?" Buckingham responded, "Other than what I expressed, that's—scientists, a lot of scientists—don't ask me the names. I can't tell you where it came from. A lot of scientists believe that back through time, something, molecules, amoeba, whatever, evolved into the complexities of life we have now."

Is our children learning?

Anyway, the trial was only about half over when this issue of *Scientific American* went to press, so we'll have to revisit it at a later date (see page 88). Hey, nobody said eternal vigilance was going to be easy.

KHA-NYOU SMELL A RAT?

TRACKING DOWN REAL ROCK RODENTS AND IMAGINARY AMAZON APES

August 2005

On May 20 I was in my office "working," a euphemism for surfing the Web, when I noticed that two articles from very different news sources had a common theme. The stories brought up many questions. Was life imitating art? Was art actually cribbing from life? If I asked my tax adviser's opinion during lunch, was the meal deductible?

In fact, lunch was what connected the two news pieces. The first story, which appeared in the *Australian* and was datelined May 19, carried the title "KEBAB MEAT RODENT A NEW SPECIES." The lead paragraph noted that "an odd-looking rodent, spotted in a food market in Laos where it was going to be turned into a kebab, has turned out to be not only a new species but also the first member of a new family of mammals to be identified in more than three decades." The rodent is known locally as kha-nyou, as well as rock rat. The article also stated that "the discovery was made by Robert

Timmins, a member of the New York–based Wildlife Conservation Society (WCS), who spotted a dead rock rat as it was about to be grilled."

I thought of comedian Lewis Black's take on Europeans seeing North American fauna for the first time—"Holy &!@%, look at that! What the @!#% is that? [Pause.] Let's eat it."—and continued Web surfing. The next stop was the *Onion*, which calls itself "America's Finest News Source," despite, or because of, the fact that it simply makes its news up. I was thus startled to see the headline "new, delicious species discovered." The *Onion* story, datelined May 18 and written in flawless wire-service style, began, "Manaus, Brazil—An international team of scientists conducting research in the Amazon River Basin announced the discovery of a formerly unknown primate species" that was "an amazing biological find" and "tastes wonderful with a currant glaze."

Further research turned up the fact that the WCS had issued a press release about the kha-nyou on May 11 and that the *Scientific American* Website actually mentioned the find on May 12. (Note to self: Holy &!@%, *Scientific American* has a Website: www.sciam.com! Let's read it.) Did the *Onion* stoop to relying on real news for its ideas, basing its Brazilian primate, "informally known as the delicacy ape," on the kha-nyou?

Answering this question was going to require true investigative journalism (which stinks because it really is work). A call to the *Onion* revealed that they had come up with the delicacy ape piece well before the kha-nyou news broke and that the timing of publication was purely coincidental. "But we could make up a story if you want us to," my source there said, in finest *Onion* fashion.

I next called Robert Timmins at his home in Madison, Wis., and found out that he had in fact beaten the *Onion* by years—he first spotted the kha-nyou in 1996. "It was very early, just after dawn," he recalled. "I was at a fresh food market, where everybody brings in their vegetables from farms, animals from the forest, fish from the river." The kha-nyou was for sale next to some vegetables. "I knew immediately it was something I had never seen before," Timmins said.

It took two years to get specimens out of Laos and another seven for Paulina Jenkins of London's Natural History Museum and C. William Kilpatrick of the University of Vermont to do a complete scientific analysis of the creature and prepare a long, detailed paper for publication in the journal *Systematics and Biodiversity*. (Taxonomy is really work.)

They gave the kha-nyou the Latin name *Laonastes aenigmamus*, in the new family *Laonastidae. Laonastes* translates to "inhabitant of the rocks of Laos." *Aenigmamus* means "riddle mouse," which "alludes to the enigmatic taxonomic position of this rodent," the journal article explains. Is it closest to the mole rats, or porcupines, or even chinchillas? That's unclear. Where would the kha-nyou itself prefer to be located? Just not next to the vegetables, thank you.

C-A-T-T-T-T-T-T-T

March 2000

"The fog comes on little cat feet," wrote Carl Sandburg. The great poet and historian may merely have been attempting to animate water vapor, but he presciently put his finger on one of modern life's more vexing problems. Feline feet can indeed induce a fog, as when you return from grabbing a cup of coffee and find that the cat has done a foxtrot all over the computer keyboard. Four furry paws can turn the "Now is the time for all good men" that was left on screen into "Now is the time for all good mennnnnbbbbbbbvccc-cccxzzzzzzzxcvbnm,;/////////ppoooo," a decidedly less co-gent, if more original, thought.

We human beings are not completely without our wiles, though. Faced with this epidemic of cat hacking, a member of our species named Chris Niswander set his mind to cat-proofing computers for the benefit of all hu-manity. What sparked his thinking, Niswander says, was his sister's cat, whose footwork crashed a running program and uninstalled some software. "It was kind of impressive," he said of the cat feat.

Niswander, a thirty-year-old software engineer and president of a Tucson software company called BitBoost, ul-timately created PawSense, a program that allegedly dis-criminates between people and cats. Should it decide that a series of strokes was most likely the footwork of a cat, PawSense cuts off further keyboard input until it is ab-solutely convinced that a person is back in charge. What-ever anthropic endeavor may have been left half-done and unsaved because of an impulsive fridge trip, mail run, or bathroom break is thus kept safe from cat curiosity.

How PawSense tells a cat from a person is, like good comedy, mostly a matter of timing. "The difference between human typing and cat typing is not that cats type gibberish," Niswander notes, because humans also type stuff that looks like gibberish, such as some odd computer language. "The way that you detect cat typing is by analyzing the combinations of key presses and the timings of those key presses in the combinations," he explains. Were I, a typical human, to describe something I've seen, I would type the letters *s, a,* and then *w.* Were I a cat attempting to share its experience of the world, however, I'd probably press those three letters simultaneously and trigger the software's alarms. Were I Hunter S. Thompson, I might find that the software stifles my creativity.

I recently tested PawSense, using a borrowed cat named Schrier. The software worked surprisingly well, blocking Schrier from her attempts to improve sketchy works of questionable literary value. Once the software makes its decision that a cat has commandeered the keys, the monitor screen turns gray and boldly warns, "Cat-Like Typing Detected." It also runs a choice of incredibly annoying sounds, such as a harmonica, bad operatic song stylings, and general hissing that, at least in theory, may drive a cat away from the computer. A human has two ways to reestablish keyboard dominion. One may type the word "human" to prove that one in fact is one. Or, based on the assumption that a cat cannot manipulate a computer mouse with anything resembling the decapitating dexterity the species exhibits with an actual mammalian mouse, a person can click a bar on screen that reads, "Let me use the computer!" An added benefit of the software is that it may train your average human to be at least a slightly better typist—I triggered the program once when I mashed a bunch of keys typing this story.

Of course, PawSense is but a stopgap. The day is dawning when voice-recognition technology will remove the keyboard from the computer-human interface. Cats may then creep on their silent haunches back to their usual haunts. Such an evolutionary development should open up a new niche: parrots seem destined to be the bane of tomorrow's computer users, with some future "BeakSense" software presumably designed to monitor obsessive use of the word "cracker."

BAIT AND SWITCH

SOME NOTES ON OUR FEATHERED AND FINNED FRIENDS

February 2006

On Thanksgiving Day, I saw a bird get stuffed. The bird was a great blue heron, *Ardea herodias*, at the Loxahatchee National Wildlife Refuge in Boynton Beach, Fla. Just after noon, the heron fired its beak into floating vegetation in a canal. He came up with a face full of foliage in the midst of which was a honking big catfish. The avian epicure thus grabbed both the salad and the sushi courses in one swell swoop.

The great blue then flew perhaps 75 yards to a sandbar, where he dropped his takeout—and checked on the state of another large fish he had apparently already caught and deposited there. (I found Web references attesting to the fact that great blues occasionally catch two fish at the same time, putting the kibosh on my claim to a bona fide scientific discovery. So, unfortunately for everyone, it's back to basement chemistry experiments.)

Great blue herons work on large prey for quite a while before the final big gulp. They repeatedly impale the fish with their beaks to soften them up, dip them in water to wet them down and orient them so that they'll slide in headfirst. Our *Ardea* alternated his attention between his two fish. Despite the holiday, there weren't any turkeys at the refuge, but a few turkey vultures did arrive to see about getting a piece of the action. The heron tried to guard both his catches but ultimately gave up his first fish to the vultures to concentrate on the fresher catfish. After almost an hour, the bird picked up his traumatically tenderized, properly positioned prize and swallowed it whole. I then went to my dad's house and pigged out, with no egrets.

In another fish tale, Vermonters got a rude surprise just after Thanksgiving. Lake Champlain sea lampreys, which chow down on tasty salmon and trout before humans can, had been "the lead villains on Vermont's 'Most Unwanted' list of invasive species," according to the *Burlington Free Press*. But genetic analysis revealed that the lamprey is in fact a Vermont native. Well, native enough—they probably got caught in the then new lake some 11,500 years ago.

The development is a particular blow to the psyche of the locals, who vaunt Vermontitude. An oft-told story concerns a Vermont couple who travel to a hospital just over the border in New Hampshire, where the wife gives birth. The next day they return home with their baby son. The boy never leaves the state again, becomes an honored citizen and passes away peacefully in his late 90s. The newspaper headlines his obituary: "New Hampshire Man Dies in Vermont."

Finally, news about the one that got away. Idaho Senator Larry Craig had a bone to pick with what's called the Fish Passage Center in Portland, Ore. According to the *Washington Post*, the center's fish counts showed that the Columbia-Snake hydroelectric system was killing salmon. And that spilling some of the water over dams rather than through turbines would buoy salmon numbers. A judge then tipped the scales in favor of the fish, but that meant utilities would take it on the chinook.

So Senator Craig—a former National Hydropower Association "legislator of the year"—then added a few words to a piece of $30-billion general legislation that simply ended the center's $1.3-million annual funding. He seized on a 2003 independent assessment of the center, which indeed did have a few criticisms. The *Post* quoted an author of the review, however, as saying that the center's work was of high technical quality and that Craig's selective quoting from the report gave a misleading impression of the reviewer's generally good opinion.

"False science leads people to false choices," Craig accurately said in defending his efforts. And no science leads to no choices. The senator's press secretary answered a reporter's question by saying that Craig wasn't being vindictive, because "that is not his style." The secretary's name, deliciously, is Whiting, speaking of fish stories.

THIS IS ONLY A TEST

AN INTERACTIVE LOOK AT SOME RECENT SCIENCE STORIES IN THE NEWS

August 2003

The dog days of August are upon us. What could be more of a distraction from the summer swelter than the shelter of a familiar exercise ordinarily reserved for the academic year? Therefore, it's time for that old favorite, the true-or-false quiz. (Don't worry, I'll write the essays.)

1. Einstein and Newton may have had a form of autism.

True, according to one autism researcher. *New Scientist* reports that Simon Baron-Cohen of the University of Cambridge thinks that the two great physicists might have had a form of autism called Asperger syndrome. Markers for the syndrome include an obsessive focus on a subject of interest, poor relationships, and communication difficulties. (But of course, those symptoms also describe millions of people who listen to hours of sports talk radio every day.) By the way, a newspaper article on Baron-Cohen's theory notes that "firm diagnosis on the dead is impossible," which I disagree with, because rigor mortis is about as firm a diagnosis as there is.

2. A seventeen-year-old boy in Nuremberg, Germany, is capable of teleportation.

False. The boys claiming to be the possessors of this extraordinary ability were really identical evil twins. One of the twins would demand money from small children, who would turn and flee for a block or so, only to run into what they took to be the very bully they'd just escaped. In May a court told the duplicate delinquents to stop doppelgänging up on people.

3. Scientists proved that an infinite number of monkeys on an infinite number of typewriters will compose the complete works of Shakespeare.

False. But researchers at Plymouth University in England showed that six Sulawesi crested macaques with access to a computer for four weeks at a zoo will produce a tale told by an idiot. According to a May wire service report, the computer was placed in the monkey enclosure, where "the lead male got a stone and started bashing the hell out of it." (A palpable hit.) "Another thing they were interested in," a researcher said, "was defecating and urinating all over the keyboard." (It smells of mortality.) They also pressed the "s" key a great deal for ssssssssome reason. The clacking macaque project was paid for with a grant from England's Arts Council, which will publish the monkey literary efforts as *Notes towards the Complete Works of Shakespeare*. The U.S. National Endowment for the Arts is rumored to be coming out with a companion volume, *Thrilled We Didn't Fund It.*

4. In April the CIA decided to classify a report on a January session in which microbiologists and the CIA's strategic assessment group discussed scientific *openness*.

True. That popping sound was your head exploding.

5. Phosphatase enzymes expedite the breakdown of phosphate monoesters in about ten milliseconds. Without the enzyme, the reaction's half-life would be a trillion years.

True. Richard Wolfenden, an enzyme maven at the University of North Carolina at Chapel Hill, and his colleagues published that finding in a recent *Proceedings of the National Academy of Sciences USA*. Here's an easy way to appreciate how long a trillion years is. If you paid off the national debt at one dollar a year, it would take 6.4 times as long as the half-life of the enzyme reaction. Fortunately, you don't have to worry about a race between exceedingly slow biochemistry and unbelievably torpid debt relief, because we're lucky enough to have enzymes, and the debt is actually getting bigger.

6. Football players at Giants Stadium in New Jersey run on old sneakers.

True. The stadium's new fake grass is made from recycled sneakers. I learned this listening to sports talk radio.

CHAPTER 2

Clearly Thinking

KABUL SESSION

A SCIENCE PRIMER FOR ANY READERS WHO RICHLY DESERVE TO GET TAUGHT A LESSON

February 2002

News media revealed last November that notes and textbooks were found in an abandoned house in Kabul that indicated that a member of the Taliban was pursuing various lines of scientific exploration. His level of expertise was judged to be at best that of an undergraduate student in chemistry and physics, which is still good enough to make stuff blow up. (Trust me. I was a chemistry major. I know.) Particularly shocking to the staff here at *Scientific American* was evidence that the Talibaner apparently read this magazine: his discarded notes included references to the so-called plasma jet, a propulsion system designed for lengthy space trips that was described in detail in an article entitled "The VASIMR Rocket," in the November 2000 issue.

If his research goal was indeed to lead the Taliban on a voyage away from Earth, well, more power to him. (With the headline on the December day I write this being "Taliban Flees Last Stronghold in Afghanistan," it would appear that many of them already took the trip, courtesy of the U.S. military.)

We must conclude, however, that he was in fact interested in using the scientific information contained in these pages for nefarious purposes. That people with bad intent read this magazine puts us in an awkward situation. Despite the potential for applications we deplore, we must continue to disseminate the most current and accurate scientific information we can, for the greater good. Therefore, the rest of this space will be devoted to the presentation of various basic facts designed to bring nasty newcomers to the study of science up to speed, which is different from velocity (and from me, because velocity has a direction).

- In Einstein's famous equation $E = mc^2$, the mc stands for the introduction of his guests for the evening.
- A watt is often the beginning of an interrogative sentence. Joules are what a nice sword is encrusted with. An erg is a desire.
- A cotyledon was a late Triassic dinosaur with a brain the size of a seed.
- 3.14159 is a large piece of pi.
- In computer language, binary code means that you owe one.
- Greenwich mean time refers to four in the morning, when the bars close in New York City's West Village.

- In electromagnetic energy, wavelength is defined as the speed of light divided by the frequency, Kenneth.
- Entomology is the other one; you're thinking of etymology.
- A Fourier transform is a mathematical manipulation by which a chinchilla turns into a coat.
- The Bernoulli principle describes a flow of air that forces Mrs. Bernoulli to sleep in the guest bedroom.
- Prime numbers are whatever Alan Greenspan says they are.
- Continental drift is when your limo wanders into oncoming traffic.
- The Nobel Prize is an award given for the year's best door knocker.
- The sine is the guy who gets a loan. The cosine is the guy who pays off the loan. The tangent is the guy in Rio who actually spends the money.
- Parthenogenesis is the creation of Greek architecture.
- Anthropology is when your uncle has to say he's sorry to his wife. (This actually happens in some places.)
- The hypotenuse is a type of syringe that holds ten shots.
- A ramjet is anyone who played football for the Rams and the Jets. The most famous ramjet is Joe Namath, who was an expert in field theory.
- The force F with which you can pound something is equivalent to m, which stands for mallet, times a, which stands for the body part into which you should pound it.

- The phalanges is a mighty river. The metatarsals are pouch-bearing mammals. And the humerus is working as hard as he can.

STICKER SHOCK

IN THE BEGINNING WAS THE CAUTIONARY ADVISORY

February 2005

Brushfires are raging all across America over the teaching of evolution, as various antievolution interests attempt to give religiously based views equal footing in science classes. These fires are fueled by so-called creation scientists, who allege that they have scientific evidence against evolution. (They don't.) Their co-conspirators, the "intelligent design" crowd, go with the full-blown intellectual surrender strategy—they say that life on earth is so complex that the only way to explain it is through the intercession of an intelligent superbeing. (They don't mention you-know-who by name as the designer, but you know who you-know-who is, and it isn't Brahma.)

One little blaze can be found in Cobb County, Georgia. As this issue of *Scientific American* went to press, a federal judge in Atlanta was in the process of deciding whether biology textbooks in the county could continue to sport a warning sticker that read: "This textbook contains material on evolution. Evolution is a theory, not a fact, regarding the origin of living things. This material should be approached with an open mind, studied carefully, and critically considered."

Maybe that last sentence should be stamped into every textbook (and some other books I can think of). And maybe they could rewrite the advisory so that it's accurate. Perhaps something like, "Variation coupled with natural selection is the most widely accepted theory that explains evolution. Evidence for evolution itself is so overwhelming that those who deny its reality can do so only through nonscientific arguments. They have every right to hold such views. They just can't teach them as science in this science class."

But why pick on evolution in the first place when there's so much to be offended by in virtually any science class? I propose that Cobb County–style stickers be placed in numerous other textbooks. Here are some suggestions:

Sticker in *Introduction to Cosmology*: "Astronomers estimate the age of the universe to be approximately thirteen billion years. If evolution ticks you off because you believe that the earth is only 6,000 years old, cosmology should really make smoke come out of your ears. There's a fire extinguisher next to the telescope."

Sticker in *Geography for Today*: "Some people believe that the earth is flat. An ant probably thinks the beach ball he's walking on is flat too. Anyway, this book says the earth is more like an oblate spheroid. Now go find Moldova on a map."

Sticker in *Earth Science*: "You are free to exercise your First Amendment rights in this class and to identify all stratigraphic layers as being 6,000 years old. We are free to flunk you."

Sticker in *Collegiate Chemistry*: "Electrons. They're like little tiny ball bearings that fly around the atomic nucleus like planets orbit the sun. Except that they're actually waves. Only what they really are are probability waves. But they do make your MP3 player run, seriously."

Sticker in *Our Solar System*: "Remember they said in chemistry class that electrons fly around the nucleus like planets orbit the sun? Some people think the sun and other planets go around the earth. You'll have a much easier time with the math if you just let everybody go around the sun, trust me."

Sticker in *Physics for Freshmen*: "We know that a lot of what's in this book is wrong, and with any luck they'll eventually find out that even more of it is wrong. But it's not so far off, it took some real geniuses to get us this close, and it's way better than nothing."

Sticker in *Creationism for Dummies:* "Religious belief rests on a foundation of faith. Seeking empirical evidence for support of one's faith-based beliefs therefore could be considered pointless. Or even blasphemous."

Sticker in *Modern Optics*: "CAUTION! Dark ages in mirror may be closer than they appear."

A BRIDGE TOO FAR

A MAN, A PLAN, A RIVER, CAMBRIDGE

November 2003
How can you tell that you're in Cambridge, Massachusetts, over Labor Day weekend with the start of classes at the Massachusetts Institute of Technology only days away? For

one thing, the streets teem with furniture-filled rental vans. Despite also carrying future physicists, these vehicles attempt to violate physical law by occupying the same space at the same time. On the other hand, a few drivers actually stop for red lights, which proves that they are not from the Boston area and are merely passing through to drop off freshmen.

How do you know this is erudite Cambridge, also home to Lesley University, Cambridge College, the main headquarters of the American Academy of Arts and Sciences, Harvard University, and Richdale A–Z Auto Service? Some checkout aisles in local supermarkets feature grammatically correct "Ten Items or Fewer" signs instead of the commonly seen "Ten Items or Less" notice. (Local folklore has it that anyone in the ten items lane carrying twenty items is either a Harvard student who can't count or an M.I.T. student who can't read.)

How can you be reasonably sure that this is Cambridge? Eavesdrop on the two guys behind you in a restaurant. They discuss quantum foam during the appetizer, contemplate human evolution with the main course, and accompany their dessert with an analysis of the fine points of an episode of *Star Trek*.

The clincher, however, is the strange and thrilling discovery I make upon consulting a map entitled "M.I.T. and Its Environs." While checking the legend to see if a destination is close enough to walk, I notice that the distance scales in familiar feet, meters, and miles have been joined by an interloper: the smoot. A little Internet research turns up the glorious history of the smoot, a unit so specific to, and well known at, M.I.T. that a map of Harvard made by the same company fails to include it. (The Harvard map ignores those newfangled meters too.)

First you need to know about the Harvard Bridge, "so named because it leads directly into the heart of MIT, which is near Harvard," notes Ken Nesmith, writing in the M.I.T. publication *The Tech* in 2001. The bridge crosses the Charles River and connects Boston with Cambridge. Now meet George Smoot, an M.I.T. graduate, famous physicist and author of the popular cosmology book *Wrinkles in Time*. George Smoot has nothing to do with the smoot.

Well, almost nothing—in an attempt to literally clear his name, George Smoot has made the history of the smoot available on his Website. It seems that in 1958 an M.I.T. freshman named Oliver R. Smoot Jr. hoped to join the Lambda Chi Alpha fraternity. Of course, inclusion in such august societies often involves ordeals that test the prospective member's fitness. Oliver Smoot's future frat brothers therefore commenced to roll him "head over heels the entire length of the bridge," according to the account published on George's site. Oliver's own version, published in *Nightwork: A History of Hacks and Pranks at MIT*, has him lying flat and being dragged. Either way, his five feet, seven inches is therefore one smoot. "Every ten smoots they calibrated the bridge, painting marks," the Web version continues. "The bridge was found to be exactly 364.4 smoots plus an ear," which was, miraculously, still attached.

Future frat pledges followed in Oliver's footsteps, handprints, etc., by repainting the ten-smoot lines. In 1987 the state announced plans to renovate the bridge, which would have smote the smoot, relegating the stripes to the stuff of nonmap legend. Local reporters tracked down Oliver, who removed himself from demarcation calibration replication consideration. Nevertheless, when I went to the bridge, I found relatively fresh ten-smoot markings, indicating that undergraduates had been active in the area in the recent past. Oliver's legacy will apparently endure. And the point, of course, is smoot.

Author's note: George Smoot won the Nobel Prize in Physics in 2006.

ABOUT THE SIZE OF IT

A CONTEMPLATION ON THE STATES OF OUR PERCEPTION

June 2002

In February and March of 2002, an Antarctic ice shelf fell apart, leaving bobbing evidence of the end of its shelf life. The disintegrated Larsen B ice shelf covered approximately 1,250 square miles, which, numerous media outlets noted, was about the size of Rhode Island. Some scientists who study our planet, which is about the size of Venus, immediately blamed global warming. Whether the cause was indeed widespread warming or merely a more geographically isolated heat-up will no doubt be a subject of discussion elsewhere. And despite the fact that the Larsen B shelf weighed about 720 billion tons, which is equivalent to the 720 billion cigarettes that the U.S. produced in 2000 if each cigarette weighed one ton, I've been thinking about less weighty stuff: namely, the practice of describing the sizes of things in terms of other things.

My interest in this obscure area of journalism began a few years ago, when I was reading an article about the environmental impact of golf courses. Par for the discourse, the writer observed that all the world's golf courses combined would cover an area one-third the size of Belgium. He then committed what I have since thought of as the Belgian waffle: he pointed out that Belgium was about the size of Maryland. Why bother with the Belgian middleman? I wondered. Why not just say that the world's golf courses cover one-third the area of Maryland? And if Maryland's surface area is about 10,461 square miles, one-third of which is 3,487 square miles, one could just as easily say that the world's golf courses cover an area about one-half the size of Hawaii (6,473 square miles). Which makes more sense anyway, because Hawaii eventually *will* be completely covered with golf courses.

Even more to the point, does Belgium or Maryland immediately conjure up a useful impression of size? The average American would be as likely to look for Belgium next to francium on the periodic table as on a map of Europe. By the way, Europe, at about four million square miles, covers an area a little bit bigger than the U.S., including Alaska and Hawaii, or including just Alaska without Hawaii. As for Maryland, it only looks big because it's all over Delaware.

Speaking of Delaware, at roughly the same time that Larsen B hit the sea came the story of an iceberg called B-22. (Coincidentally, a Mrs. Goldberg called B-22 once in a bingo game in Florida, which is about the size of Arkansas.) News accounts of B-22 busting loose from Antarctica remarked that the iceberg was about the size of Delaware. Such a description probably means that B-22 is a really big iceberg, although Delaware is a really small state. Which brings us back to Rhode Island and Larsen B.

Considering that the single most identifiable attribute of Rhode Island is that it's the *smallest* state in the union, tying the Larsen B shelf to Rhode Island may have inadvertently sent the message that gigantic portions of Antarctic ice falling away isn't such a big deal. But, as one scientist pointed out, the Larsen B collapse might signal the instability of the entire Antarctic Ross ice shelf, which, as some news reports felt compelled to reveal, is about the size of France. Changes in the integrity of the Ross ice shelf might indicate future worldwide climate changes and a rise in sea level, which in turn means that Rhode Island might someday be even smaller. And as Rhode Island goes, so goes Delaware. Not to mention Hawaii.

MEASURE FOR MEASURE

A BRIEF HOMAGE TO THE GRAMS, LITERS, INCHES, AND HOURS THAT MAKE IT POSSIBLE TO KEEP TRACK OF OUR LIVES TO AT LEAST SOME DEGREE

August 2000

"Don't forget your units, your joules!" my freshman chemistry professor used to say before every exam. Actually, he had a charming accent that made the admonition sound more like, "Dohn forgeh joor junits, joor hools," which at least partly explains why the words still ring in my ears more than two decades later. He thus reminded us students of the smelly science that without units—such as the joule, a standard quantity of energy—our test answers were meaningless. It was a good lesson. After all, 0.0648 gram of sodium chloride equals the proverbial grain of salt, a grain being an avoirdupois unit in good standing, also equal to 0.002285 ounce. But what are ten or twenty of salt, other than an extra credit question on a philosophy exam?

Units are everywhere, with the exception of the previous sentence. We're drenched with ounces, laden with pounds, bursting with inches, overrun with feet. More obscure units include the hogshead, equal to sixty-three gallons for some reason. Speaking of hogsheads, there is the joke unit the milliHelen, which is the precise amount of beauty required to launch a single ship. There are profound, poetic units: T. S. Eliot's creation Prufrock notes, "I have measured out my life with coffee spoons." And this was way before Starbucks colonized the planet.

Units are indispensable to the most mundane activities—you can't buy a quart of milk without 'em. Most of the time, however, we focus more on the thing we are measuring and not on the units by which the thing gets measured. Units thus resemble sports officials: the only time you really pay any attention to them is when something stupid happens. Bring home a pint of milk instead of the requested half-gallon, and suddenly units become the topic of conversation. Mix up the force units of pounds and newtons in calculations, and suddenly your spiffy little $125-million Mars Climate Orbiter gets lost in space.

The Mars mess-up was major. The correction of a minor units blooper recently occurred in the *New England Journal of Medicine*. First we go back to last December, when the *Journal* published a letter detailing a study that measured the number of calories expended during a favorite American activity, gum chewing. The authors needed units to keep track of their subjects' gum-chews, a word that would have sounded to my chemistry professor like Raymond Chandler describing a detective. So for chews, they chose a time-honored unit for measuring regular, periodic phenomena: the hertz (Hz). Defined as the number of cycles per second, the hertz is actually quite familiar: your AM radio dial numbers are in kilohertz, and the FM side is in megahertz.

The gum investigators blew it, however, when they noted that "the subjects were ... instructed to chew at a frequency of precisely 100 Hz (a value that approximates chewing frequency at our institution)." Taken at face value, that meant that at their institution, the prestigious Mayo Clinic, gum chewers were ripping through the Bazooka at 100 chews per second. Oh, the humanity.

The error was caught by an observant reader whose letter was published in the *Journal*'s May 18 issue. The writer realized that the researchers really meant to say their subjects chewed 100 times per minute. Which once again brings to mind Prufrock, who mused about cycles per minute: "In a minute there is time for decisions and revisions which a minute will reverse." Which brings us back to the letter, whose author is well acquainted with decisions and reversals, being not a physician but an attorney. Which leads to one last thought: lawyers who read the *New England Journal of Medicine* probably make doctors tremble in a frequency range easily expressed in hertz.

IT IS HIGH, IT IS FAR

BUT IT'S NOT GONE, BECAUSE THERE ARE SOME LAWS YOU JUST CAN'T BREAK

February 2004

As has been said often in these pages, there's a clear and present need for better math and science education in this nation. One obvious place for improvement in our math and science skills can be found among the hosts of and callers to the country's many sports talk radio programs.

Recently I was listening to a show on which the host contended that the Boston Red Sox's 2004 payroll had swelled to the point where Sox fans couldn't complain that the New York Yankees' even larger payroll gave the Yankees any advantage. A Boston caller disagreed, saying, "The Red Sox payroll is only $120 million, and the Yankees is $180 million. You know what percentage $120 million is of $180 million? Seventy-five percent." The host did not dissuade the caller. This display came from two grown men who spend an inordinate amount of their time calculating batting averages.

That exchange was about simple arithmetic. But the next morning I was treated to a lively discussion of Newtonian physics. The two morning hosts had left the subject of sports for a moment to discuss national news headlines. One story involved a Ku Klux Klan initiation ceremony at which a Klansman had fired a gun into the air. By the way, part of the radio hosts' conversation went something like this:

> "The Klu Klux Klan."
> "It's not Klu. It's Ku. It's not Klu Klux Klan, it's Ku Klux Klan."
> "I didn't say Klu Klux Klan, I said Klu Klux Klan."
> "You said it again, you said Klu."
> "I did not say Klu Klux Klan, I said Klu Klux Klan."
> "You said it again. You said Klu."

I was grateful I *didn't* have a gun. Fortunately, they eventually departed from the science of linguistics and returned to classical mechanics. As noted, some Klan member was firing a gun straight up in the air. You've probably guessed by now that a bullet came back down, which they tend to do. Well, all the bullets came back down. But one in particular found its way to the ground only after going clean through the top and then out the bottom of the skull of one of the celebrants, critically injuring him. (A British newspaper headlined this story "Ku Klux Klan Man Shot as Initiation Goes Wrong." Which raises the question: What Klan initiation has ever gone right?)

Anyway, the talk show hosts were incredulous that a bullet could have come down hard enough to do that kind of head damage "just from gravity," as one put it.

Now, I wouldn't necessarily expect Klansmen to go in for the kind of book learning that would reveal that a bullet returning to earth after being shot straight up could return fast enough to cause serious injury. What did surprise me was that two men who basically watch the trajectory of projectiles for a living—batted baseballs, for example— would be incredulous at the speed at which some objects return to earth. Hadn't they ever noticed that when a catcher fields a major league pop-up, where the baseball has gone almost straight up and down, the ball smashes into that catcher's mitt pretty darn hard?

In summary, as a public service for guys waving guns or news copy: stuff that goes up fast comes down fast. In a vacuum, where air resistance is not a factor, an object sent on a flight has a final downward speed that is, amazingly enough, equal to its initial upward speed. I've seen the equations—it's true! Closer to home, air resistance does indeed slow down a bullet or baseball, but both still gallop back to earth at quite a clip. And a bullet is pointy.

Clearly, the gunman, who has been charged with aggravated assault and reckless endangerment, did not intend to hit his victim. Why, he shot in the completely opposite direction! But ignorance of the laws of motion is no excuse. Nevertheless, the bet here is that the shooter gets off and that Isaac Newton gets charged with being an accessory after the fact. Or, actually, three centuries before.

CHECK THOSE FIGURES

HEY, IT'S PLAYTIME! ICONS—YOU CAN, TOO!

January 2004

Superman could fly faster than a speeding bullet, presumably a lot faster. But even more powerful than the caped Kryptonian was Albert Einstein, who limited Superman's flight speed to that of light. So it makes sense that Einstein, too, is now available as an action figure—think G.I. Joe with a rumpled sweater, using his kung fu grip to smash paradigms with a single equation. Or, as the catalogue sales copy has it, "Dressed for intense classroom action, this 5" tall, hard-plastic Einstein Action Figure stands with a piece of chalk in his hand, poised to explain relativity . . . Features realistic disheveled hair."

The Einstein Action Figure (it really should be a No-Action-at-a-Distance Figure, the editor in chief of this magazine helpfully pointed out) is brought to you by Archie McPhee & Co. in Seattle, which bills itself as "Outfitters of

Popular Culture. Since 1980." The McPhee action hero line includes Sigmund Freud as well as Ben Franklin, a first-rate scientist when he wasn't revolting. But no other scientists are represented. I therefore propose the creation of the following additional science action figures to round out the collection:

Barbara McClintock: "You'll jump genes with reckless abandon as McClintock plays her corny joke on the scientific establishment. Includes Nobel Prize, which arrives much, much later."

Isaac Newton: "Pelt your genius action figure with apples until he figures out the gravity of the situation. Equal-and-opposite reaction figure sold separately."

Archimedes: "'Hey, Mom, I found him!' Whether taking a bath, looking for that elusive lever long enough to move the earth or just plain screwing around, Archy metes out good times. Keep the Syracuse smarty away from Roman soldiers, and he might come up with the calculus two millennia early!"

Carl Djerassi: "He put the 'action' in action figure when he invented the birth-control pill. Now you can put him on your shelf—but don't forget to take him down the morning after!"

Edward Teller: "Ed goes fission—and fusion!—through political minefields for five decades pitching nukes. From mass destruction to nudging away incoming comets and asteroids, Edward tells ya, 'No nukes is bad nukes.'"

Lorenzo Romano Amedeo Carlo Avogadro: "What a mouthful! But you've got his number now—you'll have 6.02×10^{23} hours of fun with the man who figured out that equal volumes of all gases at the same temperature and

pressure contain the same number of molecules. No, really, you will."

The Big Box o' Steves: "What's more fun than a scientist-writer? A scientist-writer named Steve! You'll get Steven Weinberg, Stephen Jay Gould, Stephen Wolfram, Steven Pinker and Stephen Hawking. Hi-ho, Steverino! (Keep Pinker and Gould figures separate to avoid spontaneous combustion.)"

Antoine Lavoisier: "Out with the bad phlogiston, in with the good oxygen. You'll lose your head (he did, in that scary Reign of Terror!) over the man behind the law of conservation of mass. Thirteen-year-old wife not sold in the U.S."

Frans de Waal: "I see primates, I see Frans! Stare at de Waal as he observes chimps and picks up clues about why we humans do the wacky things we do. You'll have a Goodall time!"

Werner Heisenberg: "Uncertain where you left your Heisenberg action figure? So is he! Check the desk drawers. But don't be surprised if you find Schrödinger's cat. Which may be dead. Or alive!"

Charles Darwin: "This action figure loves coming along for boat rides and bird-watching but can get down at the Down house in Downe for 40 years at a time. Comes complete with his faithful bulldog, Huxley. Warning: some school boards may try to stick pins in him, but he'll survive those pricks."

I was going to suggest B. F. Skinner, but what good is an action figure you don't take out of the box?

SMART THINKING

November 2000

Here's how you know people think you're smart: they call you "Einstein." Here's how you know people think you're really smart: you're the guy whose name, Einstein, is what smart people get called. The really smart guy's name may also be used sarcastically—ya follow me, Einstein? (Quick digression: Was this habit popular throughout history? Centuries ago did anyone ever say, "You forgot to muck the stalls again, Newton." Or, "Hey, Pythagoras, your sandal's untied about halfway up your calf.")

Finally, here's how you know people think you're really, really smart: in a study designed to examine perceptions of intelligence, undergraduates consistently and often by a wide margin picked Albert Einstein in response to the instruction, "Think of an ideal example of an intelligent person." The research, performed at the University of British Columbia and recently published in the *Canadian Journal of Behavioural Science*, was designed to get a better grasp on judgments of intelligence. The authors point out that such perceptions and conceptions "influence attitudes and behavior in everyday social interactions, voting preferences . . . and can affect personnel decisions." Ask any kid whose teachers already taught that kid's older sibling.

The study examined the responses of hundreds of sophomores and juniors over a two-decade stretch, with data gathered in 1982, 1984, 1989, 1993, and 1997. Even though each student could name only one person, Einstein always topped the list and never had less than a 16 percentage

point lead over his closest rival—with the exception of 1982, when he edged Pierre Trudeau by a single point. (For you younger readers, Trudeau was the dashing, erudite Canadian prime minister who presided over Canada's final, full independence from Great Britain. His wife Margaret, apparently much more of an Anglophile than Pierre, eventually left him and wound up dating half the Rolling Stones.)

The Trudeau votes are part of a fascinating trend. Both the Canadian and British prime ministers—whoever they happened to be at the time of a particular polling—do well in the voting. And whoever is the president of the U.S. does even better. This prejudice has led to oddball assessments of brainpower in which Ronald Reagan beat Leonardo da Vinci (last superpower over *Last Supper*), George Bush the Elder topped Stephen Hawking (read my lips over try to read my books), and Bill Clinton outpolled Isaac Newton (mastication over gravitation).

The results reveal the importance of three factors in assumptions about intelligence: familiarity, likability, and power. Who could be more familiar than the prime minister or the president, both of whom probably appear on Canadian television on an almost nightly basis? And if those people didn't have a talent for being liked, chances are they wouldn't be in office in the first place.

Both familiarity and likability probably take a back seat to power, however, which explains why the Canadian P.M.'s usually finished behind the U.S. presidents. "Why aren't Canadians biased toward their own leaders?" the authors ask. "The paradox, we suspect, is based on the fact that Presidents . . . are viewed as more powerful than our

Prime Ministers—even with respect to Canadian affairs. Indeed, there is previous evidence that leader power supersedes leader likability in determining attributions of intelligence."

So caveat emptor, Cicero. Next time you're under the impression that somebody is smart, make sure it's not just charm or nuclear stockpiles that has you making that assumption. For example, other frequent high finishers include Steven Spielberg, Oprah Winfrey and Madonna. Now, these people are no doubt no dopes. But the fact that they appear in the top fifteen in multiple years, whereas John Bardeen is nowhere to be found, is a strong indicator that in conceptions of intelligence, fame and power trump (oh yeah, the Donald made the lists too) two quiet Nobel Prizes in Physics. That's right, Bardeen won two Nobels, which is one more than Einstein got. And probably at least one more than you've got, Einstein.

ANNUAL RAPPORT

LIKE A GOOD WINE, 2005 HAD A FINE FINISH

March 2006

One of the better gifts in Santa's bag is the year-end edition of the *British Medical Journal*, which brightens the cold days of late December with research reports that are actually fun to read. Take the report entitled "Harry Potter Casts a Spell on Accident Prone Children." The authors note that kid

crazes, such as skating and scootering, often lead to emergency room visits. But traumatic injury as a result of widespread *Harry Potter* reading would presumably be rare, they say, "given the lack of horizontal velocity, height, wheels, or sharp edges associated with this particular craze."

So they tracked ER visits on weekends after the release of the past two Harry Potter books and found a "significant fall," but only of the kind in which no one gets hurt. Hospital trips were halved when kids were hunkered down with Harry. The authors muse: "It may therefore be hypothesized that there is a place for a committee of safety-conscious, talented writers who could produce high-quality books for the purpose of injury prevention." The Muggles who wrote the report point out, however, that the flip side could be "an unpredictable increase in childhood obesity, rickets, and loss of cardiovascular fitness."

Another study of particular interest during the celebratory season was on the "Shape of Glass and Amount of Alcohol Poured." Seems that our brains confuse height with volume—even experienced bartenders attempting to pour a standard shot misoverestimate and actually deliver about 20 percent more alcohol into a short, wide glass than into a tall, thin one. The scientists recommend going with highball glasses to avoid overpouring or to use "glasses on which the alcohol level is marked." Now, I can't see getting a special pair of glasses to wear just for pouring drinks, but I don't entertain that much. [*Editors' note: We agree—he barely entertains us at all.*]

Perhaps the most important research turned up in "The Case of the Disappearing Teaspoons: Longitudinal

Cohort Study of the Displacement of Teaspoons in an Australian Research Institute." Noting that lounges at their institute always seemed to be short on teaspoons, which led to an inability to use sugar or instant coffee efficiently, which in turn must have had a negative effect on the quality of work, the researchers attempted to answer the question "Where have all the bloody teaspoons gone?"

The investigators planted seventy "discreetly numbered" teaspoons in the kitchen and did a weekly census. After five months, 80 percent of the teaspoons were gone, with teaspoons in common areas having a half-life of a mere forty-two days. The authors propose three explanations. Quoting the classic 1968 *Science* article "The Tragedy of the Commons," which explains how individual overuse can destroy a community asset, they note that people may actually have taken the spoons. They also suggest the possibility of a distant planet populated by spoon life-forms, to which the spoons somehow migrated. Finally, they consider the theory of counterphenomenological resistentialism—"the belief that inanimate objects have a natural antipathy towards humans, and therefore it is not people who control things but things that increasingly control people." In other words, if you still think you're running the show, well, where *have* all the bloody teaspoons gone?

The *BMJ* was joined in spreading holiday cheer by Judge John Jones. On December 20 he issued his decision in the Dover, Pennsylvania, intelligent design trial that has been frequently mentioned in this column. The decision, available on the Web, is an instant classic of science writing, not to mention jurisprudence. In addition to delineating why untestable intelligent design is equivalent to the spoon-space-travel hypothesis above, Judge Jones harangued the school board for its "breathtaking inanity" in requiring an antievolution, pro-ID statement to be read in public school science classes. Local authorities are now looking into perjury charges against pro-ID board members who apparently lied in depositions and on the witness stand. Not very intelligent.

EINSTEIN'S HOT TIME

GREAT THEORETICIANS KNOW THAT HYPOTHESIS MUST BE CONFIRMED WITH EXPERIMENT

September 2002

A well-known quote from Albert Einstein, a member of the all-time time team, is his attempt to make relativity more accessible to the layperson: "When a man sits with a pretty girl for an hour, it seems like a minute. But let him sit on a hot stove for a minute and it's longer than any hour. That's relativity."

Some serendipitous research shows that the pretty girl/hot stove line turns out to be more than just a clever musing. On a recent stroll through exceedingly dusty stacks at the local library, I stumbled upon the statement in its original form. Amazingly, the pretty girl/hot stove quote is actually the abstract from a short paper written by Einstein that appeared in the now defunct *Journal of Exothermic Science and Technology* (*JEST*, Vol. 1, No. 9: 1938). Apparently, the great theoretician tried his hand, and other body parts, at experimentation to derive his simple explanation for relativity. Here now, in its entirety, is that paper.

"On the Effects of External Sensory Input on Time Dilation."
A. Einstein, Institute for Advanced Study, Princeton, N.J.

Abstract: When a man sits with a pretty girl for an hour, it seems like a minute. But let him sit on a hot stove for a minute and it's longer than any hour. That's relativity.

As the observer's reference frame is crucial to the observer's perception of the flow of time, the state of mind of the observer may be an additional factor in that perception. I therefore endeavored to study the apparent flow of time under two distinct sets of mental states.

Methods: I sought to acquire a hot stove and a pretty girl. Unfortunately, getting a hot stove was prohibitive, as the woman who cooks for me has forbidden me from getting anywhere near the kitchen. However, I did manage to surreptitiously obtain a 1924 Manning-Bowman and Co. chrome waffle iron, which is a reasonable equivalent of a hot stove for this experiment, as it can attain a temperature of a very high degree. Finding the pretty girl presented more of a problem, as I now live in New

Jersey. I know Charlie Chaplin, having attended the opening of his 1931 film *City Lights* in his company, and so I requested that he set up a meeting with his wife, movie star Paulette Goddard, the possessor of a shayna punim, or pretty face, of a very high degree.

Discussion: I took the train to New York City to meet with Miss Goddard at the Oyster Bar in Grand Central Terminal. She was radiant and delightful. When it felt to me as if a minute had passed, I checked my watch to discover that a full fifty-seven minutes had actually transpired, which I rounded up to one hour. Upon returning to my home, I plugged in the waffle iron and allowed it to heat up. I then sat on it, wearing trousers and a long white shirt, untucked. When it seemed that over an hour had gone by, I stood up and checked my watch to discover that less than one second had in fact passed. To maintain unit consistency for the descriptions of the two circumstances, I rounded up to one minute, after which I called a physician.

Conclusion: The state of mind of the observer plays a crucial role in the perception of time.

Einstein scholars disagree, but the pretty girl/hot stove experiment also may have led to another of his pithy remarks, namely: "If we knew what it was we were doing, it would not be called research, would it?" Then again, Einstein was a bit of a wag. Consider his explanation of wireless communication: "The wireless telegraph is not difficult to understand.

The ordinary telegraph is like a very long cat. You pull the tail in New York, and it meows in Los Angeles. The wireless is the same, only without the cat." This quote reportedly kept Schrödinger awake well past his bedtime.

ONE HUNDRED YEARS OF MAGNITUDE

THE EVER LENGTHENING CURRICULUM VITAE, AND VITA, OF ERNST MAYR

August 2004

This month marks the publication of a new book, *What Makes Biology Unique?* (Cambridge University Press, 2004). Such philosophizing about science is inherently fascinating but in this case may be less interesting than the philosopher. The book is the twenty-fifth by Ernst Mayr, who was scheduled to add another significant achievement to his already prolific list shortly before this issue of *Scientific American* hit the newsstands: July 5 was Mayr's 100th birthday.

On May 10 the Museum of Comparative Zoology (MCZ) at Harvard University, Mayr's research home for the past fifty years, held a symposium/slightly premature birthday bash in his honor. I arrived early and found the Geology Lecture Hall still mostly empty. A few minutes later an exceedingly elderly gent, not Ernst, slowly ambled in and did a cost-benefit analysis on the available seats. I overheard him say to no one in particular, "I need a place close enough so I can hear but not so close that I'll be a distraction when I fall asleep." This éminence grise was later introduced to the crowd as one of Mayr's former *students*.

James Hanken, director of the MCZ, began the program by noting that "this is only the latest in a string of milestones in the long and unique life and career of arguably the greatest evolutionary biologist of the twentieth century." The greatest evolutionary biologist of the nineteenth century was Darwin, and that's it, folks, we're out of completed centuries during which evolutionary biology was a science.

In 1928 Mayr performed the first survey of the birds of New Guinea's Cyclops Mountains. Hanken recounted an anecdote that illustrates both the changed nature of biological fieldwork and Mayr's capacity for one-liners. It seems that Mayr and ornithologist Peter Alden attended a recent talk at Harvard by the naturalist and television host David Attenborough about Attenborough's attempts over many years to film bowerbirds and birds of paradise in New Guinea. "And after looking at all of these beautiful birds," Hanken said, "many of which are now endangered and highly prized and not to be even touched or breathed on, Ernst leaned over to Peter and said, 'I've eaten many of those.'"

One of the day's speakers, Mary Jane West-Eberhard of the Smithsonian Tropical Research Institute, never formally studied under Mayr but nonetheless described herself as an ipso facto student of Mayr, through reading, correspondence, and conversation. Under that definition, Mayr's students number in the hundreds of thousands. She noted that for the auspicious occasion, "I thought of making a great big birthday cake. But then it occurred to me that a cake with that many candles might be regarded as a fire hazard and maybe a terrorist threat."

Mayr himself, nattily dressed and sporting a mischievous smile, expressed his "tremendous gratitude to so many people who made my life productive and enjoyable" and noted that many of those people didn't even know they were helping him. For example, he specifically thanked the woman in England who blackmailed Lord Walter Rothschild and drove him into the bankruptcy that in turn forced him to sell his bird collection to the American Museum of Natural History in New York City, where it became available for study by Mayr, who began working there in 1932.

During her talk, West-Eberhard revealed that Mayr had once shared with her one of his secrets for longevity, which was "to walk an hour a day, even when you're busy." Ever a pragmatist, Mayr was clever enough to use time and not distance as the goal. If you live long enough, you can fulfill the hour requirement simply by walking to the mailbox, which is what Mayr was doing when I arrived at his home in Bedford, Massachusetts, for a visit on the Saturday after the symposium. He spoke for almost two hours about modern biology, evolutionary theory, and his scientific life.

Author's note: Ernst passed away peacefully on February 3, 2005.

FOUNDING FATHER OF INVENTION

NOW IS THE TIME FOR ALL GOOD MEN AND WOMEN TO REFLECT FOR A MOMENT ABOUT ONE OF THE KEY FIGURES IN AMERICAN INVENTIVENESS

October 2000

Three out of every four years autumn brings crisper air, breathtaking foliage and, barring a strike, a World Series. Well, technically, it's four out of four years, but every fourth year those pleasant things are drowned out by the trumpeting elephants and braying asses of the presidential election circus. (Although I write these words in early August, I have no doubt that by the time you read them you're feeling completely bushed and totally gored.)

In the heat—well, warmth—of this historic moment, perhaps it would be refreshing to contemplate a previous occupant of the White House and reflect upon his immortal words: "It occurred then that this globe might be made to perform the functions of a dial. I ascertained on it two poles, delineated its equator and tropics, described meridians at every 15 degrees from tropic to tropic, and shorter portions of meridian intermediately for the half hours, quarter hours, and every five minutes." Thus did Thomas Jefferson describe part of his design for a spherical sundial, which, for the benefit of the current crop of presidential aspirants, is like a big watch that works only during the daytime.

When he wasn't busy thinking up the United States, Jefferson was coming up with all kinds of useful devices. He mathematically deduced an improved plow that cut through the soil with increased efficiency. He thought up a contraption, called a wheel cipher, that could encode secret written messages for safe passage to American agents overseas. And he originated channel surfing, or at least the 18th-century version, when he designed a revolving stand that enabled the busy reader to keep five books in play simultaneously. (Note to George W.: Five! Books! Hey, it's still fun to spin.)

Jefferson never bothered to patent his various inventions, as he had mixed feelings about ownership of intellectual property that might limit its dissemination. And he could afford to have such mixed feelings, being more upper crusty than the homemade apple pie he was as American as. But he also recognized that the economic motivation of at least temporary ownership of a concept for a device would spur invention. (Note to Al Gore: Nice try with the I-invented-the-Internet thing.)

So it came to pass that one of the most important things Jefferson helped to invent was the U.S. Patent Office, in 1790. As secretary of state under the original George W., Jefferson led the three-man board that reviewed patent applications. Although a big fan of inventions who went so far as to personally test some of the new devices for which patents were sought, Jefferson kept grumbling something to the effect of, "Hey, I'm the secretary of state here." In 1793 Congress finally heard his grouses, which sometimes roamed the woods around Monticello, and absolved him of his patent responsibilities. Of course, not all patents have gone to inventions as useful as those Jefferson himself dreamed up. "The abuse of frivolous patents," he once noted, "is likely to cause more inconvenience than is countervailed by those really useful." He most likely then would have disapproved of patent number 5971829, which was given to the inventor of the motorized ice cream cone. This gem of an idea rotates the scoop of vanilla so that the eater can simply stick his or her tongue out, as if entering the voting booth on November 7. Jefferson probably would also have been unhappy about patent number 5457821, granted to the guy who put a white, irregular brim together with a yellow dome to create a baseball cap that looks like a fried egg. Putting the egg on your face approximates the effect of walking out of that same voting booth.

CRIME SCENE INSTIGATION

TV SUPERSCIENTISTS AFFECT REAL COURTS, CAMPUSES AND CRIMINALS

May 2005

Television's troika of *CSI* shows—*CSI: Crime Scene Investigation, CSI: Miami,* and *CSI: NY*—arguably presents popular culture's most positive view of scientists since the Professor was engaged in his unfunded better-living-through-coconut-chemistry project on *Gilligan's Island.* In February 2005, at the annual meeting of the American Association for the Advancement of Science in Washington, D.C., a group of real forensic scientists put the *CSI*s under the microscope.

The fictional series have inadvertently put pressure on real-life prosecutors. " 'The CSI effect' is a term that came into use around 2003, when the show really started to become popular," says trace evidence analyst Max Houck, director of West Virginia University's Forensic Science Initiative. "It represents the impossibly high expectations jurors may have for physical evidence." Prosecutors worry that without having the ironclad physical evidence jurors see on TV, the reasonable-doubt line may be shifting.

Houck pointed to a case in Los Angeles last year featuring a bloody coat. "Jurors were alarmed," Houck says, "because no DNA testing had been done on the coat. Well, the wearer of the coat admitted to being at the murder scene trying to help the victim, so the lab had said there was no reason to test it—he said he was there." According to Houck, the judge made a statement along the lines that "TV has taught jurors about DNA tests but not about when to use them."

Indeed, many people still don't know the ABCs of DNA. A lab may request a sample of a missing person's clothing in order to compare DNA on that clothing to unidentified remains. Dress shirts are particularly good at grabbing skin cells at the tight collar. "We asked for the family to send in dress shirts," recalls Demris Lee of the Armed Forces DNA Identification Laboratory about one case. "And the family sent in his new shirts that were still in packaging. They couldn't believe we wanted his dirty clothes."

Criminals may be feeling *CSI*'s heat—and taking notes. "What I've heard is that it's closely watched in prisons," remarks Richard Ernest, a forensic firearms expert in Fort Worth, Tex. "And prisons become almost like a crime school for certain individuals. They'll look at a particular segment and say, 'So that's how they caught me. Well, I won't make those mistakes again.' "

Instead they'll probably make new ones. "When they try to escape detection from what they see on *CSI*, they're actually leaving more evidence," Houck contends. "A good example of that is instead of licking an envelope [for fear of providing DNA in their saliva] they'll use adhesive tape. Well, they'll probably leave fingerprints on the tape, and it'll pick up hairs and fibers from the surroundings. So the more effort you put into trying to evade detection, honestly, the more evidence you leave behind."

Another CSI effect is that college kids think it's cool. In 1999 Houck's institution graduated four students with a concentration in forensics. "We're now the largest major on campus," he declares. "If you add all four years together, we have over 400 students." Perhaps their most important lesson is that real life doesn't look like a TV show. Houck tells his students that "it's less about wearing leather pants and driving Hummers than it is about wearing Tyvek jumpsuits and crawling under people's front porches looking for body parts. Honest. I've never worn leather pants in my life."

Houck also has a tough time watching his TV counterparts use analytical tools that don't quite really exist. "We joke that we need to get one of those—that's a damn fine instrument," he says. (The amazing databases employed on some episodes prompted a friend of mine to ask, "Why don't they just ask the computer who did it?") Another show convention that annoys Houck is investigators wandering around dark indoor crime scenes. "They always use flash-lights," Houck notes. "I don't know why. I usually just turn the lights on."

•ᐧᐯ

NOSTRILDAMUS

IN SPACE, NO ONE CAN HEAR YOU GAG. WHICH IS WHY YOU NEED PREDICTIONS ABOUT WHETHER SPACE STUFF STINKS

June 2001

Musky, floral, "etheral," camphoraceous, minty, pungent, and putrid. No, these are not the names of the Seven Dwarfs before they went Hollywood. Rather they are the seven scents by which NASA calibrates and certifies the nose of George Aldrich every three months. If everything is up to snuff, George Aldrich smells.

At the White Sands Test Facility in Las Cruces, New Mexico, Aldrich and other volunteers put their noses to the grindstone and smell materials destined for spaceflight. First, rigorous instrumental analysis determines whether any gases coming off these objects are toxic or carcino-genic. (Coincidentally, Aldrich does these tests as well, in his role as a chemistry laboratory technician.) Once the gases are deemed safe, Aldrich and a four-colleague "odor panel" sniff the stuff. They decide whether the object would make an astronaut die for an open window, which is exactly what would happen 200 miles up.

Aldrich is the dean of about twenty-five smelling em-
ployees at White Sands, ranging from secretaries to engineers, who rotate in groups of five to lend NASA their noses.
He started smelling back in 1974 and had lived through a
record 743 "smell missions"—over 100 more than anyone
else as of early April 2001, when we spoke.

When a sample comes up for review, Aldrich and his co-
panelists smell it and then rank the rankness from 0 to 4. "0
is a nondetect," he explains, "1 is barely detectable, 2 is easily detectable, 3 is objectionable, and 4 is get-me-out-of-
here." Officially, 4 is "offensive." One may wonder why
NASA has not switched to some high-tech electronic nose
or to the supersensitive snouts of dogs. "We're a screening
test for astronauts, and they're human," Aldrich points out,
"so they want to use human subjects." Not to mention the
fact that some dogs might rate a dead squirrel on a sizzling
Albuquerque highway as a 2, with the additional comment,
"Needs one more day." Electronic noses are getting better
[see "Plenty to Sniff At," by Mia Schmiedeskamp, *Scientific
American*, March 2001], Aldrich notes, "but they can't tell
you if an odor will leave an aftertaste in the back of your
throat."

An aftertaste was just one bad thing about some Velcro
straps that got hurried up to the space station in February
without the all-important olfactory evaluation. The smell,
reminiscent of your fingers after slicing onions, almost
made the astronauts launch their lunch. "One of the astronauts opened the bag that these straps were in," Aldrich
says. "It stunk. He zipped the bag right back up and put it
back on the shuttle. They brought it to us, and we basically

agreed. It stunk." (The nefarious funk most likely emanated from the compound used to bond the backing to the straps.)

Aldrich recently nosed his way into being a judge at the annual Odor-Eaters Rotten Sneaker contest, held in Vermont in March. The winner this year was unquestionably eleven-year-old Rebekah Fahey, also of Las Cruces. To anyone smelling a New Mexican fix, Aldrich explains that Fahey was truly committed to victory: "She'd worn the same socks for three months. It just completely knocked me back. I asked for oxygen."

Some men are born great, some become great, and some have greatness thrust up their noses. "Everybody thinks that I have this big schnozz," Aldrich remarks. "People say, 'Thank goodness I took a bath today.' But I tell everyone I may be average to slightly above average." Well above average is his willingness to endure, ad nauseam, people in effect asking, "Does this smell funny to you?" Thanks to him and his fellow smellers, astronauts in space can breathe a little easier.

METEORWRONGS

SOME PEOPLE ARE STUCK BETWEEN A ROCK AND A HARD TRUTH

March 2005

Trains are better than planes, if you have the time and dry land. I was reminded how much I prefer trains as I waited for one on a frigid December day in Waterbury, Vermont—

a window of the tiny station featured a quaint and charming photo exhibit of great local train crashes. I haven't checked every square foot of LaGuardia Airport, but I bet there isn't a single display of entertaining and nostalgic photos of great aviation disasters.

Crashes were all over the news around the time of my train trip, because a hunk of matter some 400 meters across had suddenly become a solar system media star: the likelihood that an asteroid dubbed 2004 MN4 would cause a really bad day in the year 2029 was briefly rated an unprecedented 4 (out of 10) on the Torino scale. Contrary to popular opinion, the Torino scale is not used to weigh muscle cars coming off the Ford assembly line. The scale in fact describes the level of threat from space stuff smashing into Earth. (Imagine the current and confusing color-coded terror alert system, only with numbers and for the most part based on the best available data.)

A Torino 4 translates to "a 1 percent or greater chance of collision leading to regional devastation." A 4 also means that astronomers are confident that more data will show a lesser threat. And when more data were evaluated a few days later, the consensus was that 2004 MN4 would miss us altogether, leaving us to find our own techniques for regional devastation.

Just a few months before 2004 MN4 had everyone figuring out how old they'd be in 2029, I had visited with the inventor of the Torino scale. Richard P. Binzel, a planetary scientist at the Massachusetts Institute of Technology, has a strong affection for Pluto, amateur astronomers and the Italian city of Torino, where he first proposed the impact scale at a conference in 1999. ("A 4 on the Binzel" sounds too much like a craps-table side bet, so they went with "Torino scale.")

Binzel revealed that he regularly entertains visitors convinced that they own a piece of outer space. "The basic story is that you get a phone call where someone says that they have found a meteorite or they have just inherited this meteorite that has been in the family for generations," Binzel said. "It's a family heirloom. But to their knowledge, it's never been reported to any scientific authority. And they would like it checked out, because if it's scientifically interesting they want the scientists to know about it, and maybe it's an important case."

An alleged meteorite may have been *displayed* in an important case. For example, the most memorable sample that showed up in Binzel's office was incorporated into a redesigned bowling trophy. "Instead of the guy in the trophy holding a bowling ball," Binzel recalled, "he was holding this rock. Like Atlas. Mounted and on the mantle for generations."

But despite the hopes and expectations of their owners, the fifty or so rocks Binzel has examined for civilians have turned out to have earthy origins. "In fifteen years, no one has ever had [an] actual meteorite," he said. "So I'm careful to warn people that it's very likely they're going to walk out knowing it's not a meteorite." (A guest may still leave clutching something extraterrestrial, however—Binzel has on occasion rewarded the star-unstruck visitor with a tiny shard of an actual meteorite for his or her trouble.) And, Binzel noted, "to the credit of these people, they say, 'That's okay, all I want to know is the truth.' I've always been impressed by that."

Imagine millions of people letting go of a cherished belief simply because they're confronted with indisputable facts to the contrary. Well, before I go all John Lennon, I must say that even only fifty people able to incorporate reality into their worldview isn't bad. In fact, it fills me with a kind of hope for the future I haven't felt since the 2029 fly by of MN4 was downgraded to a 0 on the Torino scale.

OUT OF THIS WORLD

ONE UFO EXPERT SAYS THAT ALIENS DON'T GET AROUND MUCH ANYMORE. BUT WHAT IF THAT'S JUST WHAT THEY WANT YOU TO THINK?

July 2001

The sun, or perhaps some other star that warms intelligent beings light-years from Earth, has set on a venerable English institution. After half a century of inspired eccentricity, the British Flying Saucer Bureau has closed the pod bay doors. It has ceased to be. It has expired. It is pushing up crop circles. It is an ex-bureau. The reason: the bureau has virtually stopped receiving reports of flying saucers.

A family enterprise, the bureau was the 1953 brainchild of the late Edgar Plunkett and his son Denis (which makes Denis both the bureau's father and brain-brother). At the height of alien activity, the Plunketts fielded some thirty reported sightings a week, and the bureau claimed about

1,500 members scattered around the world, if not beyond. But now no one seems to be reporting UFOs.

According to the *Times* of London, Plunkett believes that the drop-off in close encounters may have a reasonable explanation: perhaps the aliens have completed their survey of Earth. One can sympathize with such an interpretation. My own home, for example, has been blessedly elephant-free lo these many years, clearly the result of some incredibly efficacious antielephant spray. With an abiding faith in Occam's new MACH3 razor—one blade tugs on loopy logic while the second blade cuts it off, leaving the third blade to skate on exceptionally thin ice— I propose other possible explanations for the downturn in UFO reports:

- The aliens have finally perfected their cloaking technology. After all, evidence of absence is not absence of evidence (which is, of course, not evidence of absence). Just because we no longer see the aliens doesn't mean they're not there. Actually, they are there; the skies are lousy with them, they're coco-butting one another's bald, veined, throbbing, giant heads over the best orbits. But until they drop the cloak because they've got some beaming to do, we won't see them.
- Sightings are as frequent as ever; people are merely neglecting to report them. With 401(k)s threatening to leave impact craters, no one is interested in aliens unless Alan Greenspan is one.

- People are still seeing them, but the aliens have administered a mass posthypnotic suggestion: "When you start to think of aliens, immediately switch to thinking about mad cow disease."
- The aliens have cleverly designed their ships to look just like standard commercial aircraft, thus explaining the massive delays at LaGuardia airport. (Newark airport is alien-free, the extraterrestrials having avoided New Jersey since the Grovers Mill snafu of '38.)
- The aliens are indeed gone, but the idea that they could complete their survey of Earth in a mere fifty years is both ludicrous and insulting. In fact, they ran out of alien government funding. Besides, a lot of the aliens back on their home planet thought that the missions to Earth were just a big hoax anyway.

These alternatives should buoy Denis Plunkett's continued belief in extraterrestrial interlopers. "I am just as enthusiastic about flying saucers as I always was," he told the *Times*, "but the problem is that we are in the middle of a long, long trough." Assuming "trough" means "lull," my calculations indicate that he shouldn't give up so easily. The bureau started in 1953, so being in the middle of the trough means that UFO sightings should be peaking no later than 2049. If by "trough," however, Denis means "feedbox," we should climb out immediately. Especially if there are any stray copies of that alien best-seller *To Serve Man* lying around.

SOYUZ WANNA FLY IN SPACE

July 1999

Anybody who goes anywhere without a roll of duct tape is a fool. This is common knowledge. It's also the second thing I thought of when I heard that a British businessman was angling for a ride on board the Mir space station, which at this point is barely even a mere space station. The first thing I thought of, as always, was my own name: Mirsky. My obsessive-compulsive desire to tack a suffix onto Mir skates through my head each time I see that three-letter word, a reaction that even I begin to find tiresome.

Anyway, the Russians, no longer Red, are in the red—which, after throwing off the shackles of communism, is like having an irony curtain descend on them. And Mir's keeping them there, with its operating costs of about $20 million a month. (In case you're wondering, $20 million converted to rubles equals one really stupid monetary transaction.) They were getting ready to scuttle Mir, skint as they are. But on January 22, 1999, they announced that they would keep Mir skyborne until 2002 if private investors would sponsor the station's upkeep.

According to wire service reports, a British businessman stepped up with an offer of $100 million, in return for which he would spend a week on Mir. Schemes from the past in which he had allegedly failed to come across with promised funding then surfaced. (The businessman will remain nameless, as *Scientific American*'s lawyers are all at their summer cottages and left strict instructions that they not be disturbed until after Labor Day.) Again according to published reports, he in turn then denied that he was ever going to be giving any money to the Russians. Instead his idea is to spend the week doing some kind of demented space-a-thon, raising money per mile traveled, which would go toward building a hospital.

As this issue went to press, Mir's key problem, the funding to keep flying, was still unsolved. Because the space station is close to my heart, however, I would like to help. And I think I have a plan at least worth considering. For one thing, I don't want to go up there, so that should help keep Mir's skyrocketing costs down. One of the supreme ironies of our time is that in space, there's so little space. If I want to spend a week in a cramped, uncomfortable, moving room that must have accumulated some interesting smells by now, I can do that for the $1.50 entrance fee to the New York City subway. (Trust me, space is not necessarily the final frontier.) For another thing, money is only as good as what you can buy with it. And I have some items I'm ready to donate to the cause, items that might be worth more than money.

Foremost on my list is one of those pens that can write upside down. The packaging even has on it, "Selected by NASA," which would make it perhaps the most reliable piece of equipment on board. The pen could be used, for example, to create a sign saying "Please send oxygen," to be held up to the window in case the space shuttle happened by.

I also have a "space blanket," one of those high-tech silvery-looking things they throw on marathon runners after the race. It's thin and light and should keep any of Mir's skilled denizens warm in case of heating system failures or unexpected misorientations away from the sun.

I have an old stationary bicycle that could serve double duty as gyroscope and power generator. The rider of that bike on board Mir, skimming over the atmosphere, could lay claim to having gotten nowhere faster than anyone in history.

Finally, I have a sleeve of Styrofoam cups. Combined with some PVC tubing and sweatsocks, both of which are probably already up there, these cups could no doubt be fashioned into a highly efficient carbon dioxide filter, based on what I remember from watching the movie *Apollo 13*.

All I ask in return for these goods is that the Russians change the name. Please.

—Steve Mir . . . sky

AND SCIENCE FOR ALL

THE SECOND LAW TRUMPS THE TENTH AMENDMENT

January 2006

Sam Alito—not the town across the Golden Gate Bridge from San Francisco, that's Sausalito—is the new nominee for associate justice of the U.S. Supreme Court. Harriet Miers had been the nominee, but she thought *Marbury v. Madison* had something to do with New York Knick point guard

Stephon Marbury and his home court of Madison Square Garden. Despite her lack of experience in constitutional law, Miers was defended by some commentators who posited that corporate law experience would come in handy when the court hears business cases. Fair enough. But surely the court will hear more and more cases involving science and technology, too. Therefore, I'd like to suggest a few science-related questions that members of the Senate Judiciary Committee might ask Supreme Court nominees:

1. What's the difference between RNA and the NRA?

2. It has been said that gravity is not just a good idea, it's the law. Is gravity indeed the law? Is gravity indeed a good idea in a land of rampant obesity?

3. What's the second law of thermodynamics? What's the third law of motion? Who's on first?

4. A related question: In his confirmation hearings, Chief Justice John Roberts compared being a judge with being a baseball umpire. Is it time for the instant replay in baseball? And does antediluvian refer to baseball prior to the *Flood* decision?

5. Do you believe in spontaneous human combustion, or do you refuse to answer on the grounds that you might incinerate yourself? (The kids, they love that one.)

6. In commenting on the death penalty, Justice Antonin Scalia said, "For the believing Christian, death is no big deal." Is death, in fact, a big deal? And if death isn't a big deal, why is murder?

7. Original *Law and Order*, or *Law and Order: Criminal Intent*?

8. Le Chatelier's principle holds that if you kick a chemical system that has settled into a dynamic equilibrium, it

will react by adopting a new equilibrium. Is kicking a system in equilibrium a violation of the Eighth Amendment's prohibition of cruel and unusual punishment?

9. How can you have deregulation that lowers product safety standards at the same time as tort reform that limits awards for injuries from unsafe products and still keep a straight face?

10. Are you a strict constructionist, holding that the Constitution is a "dead" document? If so, would it be unconstitutional to transport the original Constitution across state lines in a car but constitutional to do so by horse? Also, the element helium was discovered after the Constitution was written. Can I still use it in balloons?

11. If Justice Ruth Bader Ginsburg leaves Washington, D.C., heading west at 60 miles per hour and Justice Anthony Kennedy leaves Los Angeles heading east at 70 miles per hour, will they meet before Justice Clarence Thomas asks a question?

12. Einstein showed with relativity that different observers, depending on their relative motion, may see two events as being simultaneous or as one preceding the other. Does that, like, blow your mind? And how should it come into play when evaluating eyewitness accounts?

13. Would you use Microsoft Word to write an opinion in a case involving Microsoft?

14. In the recently concluded Scopes-like trial of *Kitzmiller v. Dover School District*, one of the defendants claimed not to know the source of the funds for 60 copies of an intelligent-design book, which he admitted to only

having glanced through, for the school library. He was then confronted with his own canceled check. Should such a defendant face charges of perjury or, despite the Eighth Amendment implications, be forced to actually read the book?

CHAPTER 3

In Sickness and in Health

HE SHOOTS, HE SCARS

October 1997

The marathon known as the National Hockey League regular season is about to begin. Hundreds of robust young warriors will soon find themselves, at one time or another, writhing in agony. A recent report in the *American Journal of Sports Medicine*, "Predictors of Injury in Ice Hockey Players," notes that "injuries are attributed to collisions with players skating at speeds up to thirty miles per hour, pucks traveling at 100 miles per hour, sharp skates, and long sticks." Well, put *Lord of the Flies* on ice, and, yes, people are going to get hurt.

Sport entails risk. The collisions common to hockey and other contact sports often cause the temporary brain-scrambling known as concussion. A review in *Medicine & Science in Sports & Exercise* with the coy title "Were You Knocked Out?" provides a summary of concussion management. It includes a list of questions to be asked as a "post-concussion memory assessment," to help determine a player's wooziness coefficient. This list includes "Which team are we playing today?" and "How far into the quarter is it?" As a rule of dislocated thumb, trainers should note that a concussed New Yorker who responds to any question with "Who wants to know?" is totally coherent.

Speaking of concussions, boxers are obviously at great risk for becoming unconscious. The infamous Mike Tyson–Evander Holyfield rematch showed that boxing's risks now include rabies. Tyson, who felt he had been wronged by a Holyfield head butt, was perfectly free to take revenge by pummeling Holyfield in the face. Other sports discourage this form of retaliation, but in boxing, heck, it's the whole point. Tyson instead decided to attempt to bite off Holyfield's ears. Because repeated concussions can cause long-term brain damage, the possibility exists that any prior incidents may have taken their toll on Iron Mike's iron head.

Speaking of irons, even pastoral sports such as golf have their risks, some of which likewise include sticking things in your mouth. The journal *Gut* has reported that a sixty-five-year-old retiree who golfed daily came down with hepatitis. Doctors searching for the cause discovered that he licked his balls before putting. This habit exposed the golfer to Agent Orange, a pesticide used on the course, and made him the first proved victim of—deep breath now—Golf War Syndrome.

Lousy golfers face other hazards. A study published a couple of years back in the *New England Journal of Medi-*

cine found that bad players in a Tennessee retirement community were more likely to get the tick-borne disease ehrlichiosis. Presumably, they spend more time in tick-ridden woods and high grass looking for errant tee shots. "What's your handicap, Arnie?" "Why, the fever and muscle aches, Jack!" (This reporter recently played a round of golf in which, for the first time, he didn't lose a single ball. Perhaps still impaired from a baseball concussion some quarter of a century ago, however, he did finish minus a sand wedge.)

Golf is for the faint of heart compared with the rough-and-tumble action reported in a *Journal of the Royal Society of Medicine* article, "A Survey of Croquet Injuries." Although wrist, hand, or forearm problems were not uncommon, croquet also leads to more serious harm. "Falling as a result of standing on a ball had the worst effects," the researcher notes. One player broke a foot bone "putting on a Wellington boot"; another "suffered a black eye from being struck on the head by a mallet."

The difference then between croquet and boxing? Mishaps of the Three Stooges variety in croquet are accidental. Tyson earned the sobriquet "Madman!" from *Sports Illustrated* for biting Holyfield. For administering a concussion, on the other hand, he would have been called "Champion!" Go figure.

THE OPEN-HEART OPEN

CARDIAC PATIENTS MIGHT WANT TO CONSIDER THE LINKS—AND NOT THOSE OF THE SAUSAGE VARIETY

January 2001

"Working too hard," pop singer Billy Joel once warned, "can give you a heart attack-ack-ack-ack-ack-ack." You ought to know by now, however, that playing too hard also may be hazardous to your health, especially for those with a history of cardiac problems. One of the challenges facing heart patients is to engage in physical activity strenuous enough to impart beneficial cardiovascular effects without being so vigorous as to impart death.

Fortunately, German researchers at the Center for Cardiovascular Diseases in Rotenberg and at the Institute for Sports Medicine at the University of Giessen have possibly pinpointed the proper pastime. As they reveal in last October's issue of *Medicine and Science in Sports and Exercise*, it is, surprisingly enough, golf, which is called golf, it's been said, only because the other four-letter words were already taken.

Of course, golf and medicine have a long history, but the connection has been for the most part related to an inability for patients to schedule Wednesday afternoon appointments. To gauge golf's appropriateness as medicine, the researchers put together a special event. "After written informed consent was obtained," they report, "twenty male golfers with cardiac diseases and eight healthy controls participated in a golf tournament after their examination in the hospital," which sounds like a typical weekend on the PGA Senior Tour. In fact, however, the intrepid golfers in the Infarct Invitational one-upped the geezer pros: the test subjects schlepped their own clubs on handcarts, thus adding to their workout.

The researchers comment that suitable physical activity for heart patients should reduce cardiovascular risk factors, increase endurance and help to reintegrate patients socially. They suspected that golf could be ideal because the handicapping system allows players of all levels and ages to compete together and because the game poses physical challenges such as walking and other coordinated movements. The investigators also cryptically note that trauma risk is minor "unless the rules and etiquette are violated," a possible veiled reference to those rare occasions when a golfer ignores the ball and swings instead at a gabby opponent.

In addition, substantial mental issues make golf more difficult than it might appear. Some golfers can't tee off if anyone watches them, which pretty much rules out playing the big-money televised tournaments. Many develop the "yips," a case of nerves that transforms a smooth putting stroke into what looks like a cross between water divination and an attempt to kill a rat with a shovel. Participants in the Cardiac Classic were faced with an additional psychological stress: "Before the competition," the researchers explain, "the golfers were informed that the winners would receive valuable prizes," which might ordinarily mean a new car but in this case could be nitroglycerin.

In another wrinkle that separated the heart study from more mundane golf outings, players had their heart rate recorded the entire time and their blood pressure measured after every three holes. Although continuous blood pressure monitoring would have been preferable, the study's authors decided against it "in order not to disturb the golf swing," thereby preventing incidents such as:

Pffft, pffft, pffft, pffft, pffft.

"Do you mind?"

"Sorry."

Now, I don't actually know much about golf, although I did once fade a six-iron with tour sauce onto an elevated dance floor and drain the bird to take a nassau. Despite my ignorance, I was fascinated to learn about the German study, especially as it dovetailed with another recent finding—according to a report in the journal *Circulation*, patients who kept physically active after a first heart attack had a 60 percent lower risk of subsequent attacks than their sedentary counterparts.

Whether healthy golfers benefit from the eighteen-hole hike remains unclear. But based on the data compiled during the tournament, golf indeed appears to have the potential to make coronary patients hearty, as in fewer ventricular arrhythmias, and hale, as in Irwin. For the cardiac-conscious, golf as exercise is thus much like the third bear bed sampled by Goldilocks: neither too hard nor too soft, but just right.

HOOP GENES

August 1998

You know how close I came to playing professional basketball? About seventeen inches. Seventeen inches taller, and I would have been an even seven feet, which at least would have given me a shot at seeing just how close a shave Michael Jordan gets on the top of his head. Having immense strength, acrobatic agility, catlike coordination, unbridled desire, and a soft touch on my fall-away jumper would also have come in handy, but the height thing couldn't have hurt. All of which brings us to genes.

Although the Human Genome Project will probably fail to uncover a DNA sequence governing three-point shooting, British researchers have indeed found a jock gene. The gene in question, which comes in two forms called *I* and *D* (for "insertion" and "deletion"), is for angiotensin-converting enzyme (ACE), a key player in modulating salt and water balance, blood vessel dilation, and maybe more. People carrying the *D* form are perfectly normal but will probably be at home watching television reports of people who have the *I* form planting flags on the top of Mount Everest.

"We got into this system because it was thought to control heart growth," says Hugh E. Montgomery of the University College London Center for Cardiovascular Research, who is the lead author of the ACE gene study, which appeared in the May 21, 1998, issue of *Nature*. "We started looking at exercising athletes purely because their hearts grow when they exercise." Assuming that a crucial factor in endurance would be efficient use of oxygen, Montgomery and his colleagues tested "extreme endurance athletes exposed to low oxygen concentrations," namely mountaineers, all of whom were also British. (Why did the British researchers test British mountain climbers? Because they were there.)

Montgomery's group found a disproportionately high representation of the *I* form among elite mountaineers, some of whom had repeatedly climbed to 8,000 meters (over 26,000 feet) without supplemental oxygen. In another study, they followed seventy-eight army recruits through a ten-week training program. Those with *I* and *D* forms tested equally before the workouts began, but soon the *I*s had it. All the exercisers increased their endurance, as measured by curls of a fifteen-kilogram (thirty-three-pound) barbell, but *I* folks improved eleven times more than the *D*s.

The studies bring to mind the eerie case of Eero Maentyranta, winner of three cross-country skiing gold medals at the 1964 Winter Olympics in Innsbruck. In 1993 researchers found that Maentyranta and a lot of his family have a genetic mutation affecting red blood cell production. As a result, Maentyranta's blood carries up to 50 percent more hemoglobin than an average male's. And whereas having, say, a third lung might get you disqualified from competition, a set of genes that grants you access to half again as much oxygen as the competition is still legal.

Biology's newfound ability to spot individual genes associated with athleticism is intriguing but, on contemplation, not surprising. "Athletics, by already selecting for extreme phenotypes, must be selecting for a significant genetic influence," says Philip Reilly, executive director of the

Shriver Center for Mental Retardation in Waltham, Mass., a clinical geneticist and an attorney who has spent the past twenty-five years pondering genetics and its implications for society. "In one sense, this is old news," he notes. "There is no physical trait for which we have better evidence of substantial genetic contribution to ultimate expression of phenotype than height." And for most athletes, jockeys being the ridiculously obvious exception, being big is advantageous. (The late, great sportswriter Shirley Povich actually bemoaned all the tallness. "[Basketball] lost this particular patron back when it went vertical and put the accent on carnival freaks," he wrote. "They don't shoot baskets anymore, they stuff them, like taxidermists.")

So genes for robust physical traits help make for a good athlete. But the basis for behavior, which also contributes to athleticism, remains more mysterious. Another forty-five army recruits, with the same proportion of *I* and *D* forms as the seventy-eight who trained for ten weeks, dropped out entirely to go home. "Sometimes," Montgomery explains, "they just miss their mums."

DIAMOND REFLECTIONS

April 1999

Who better than Roald Hoffmann to share my symmetry theory with, I thought. Hoffmann, professor of chemistry at Cornell University, is one of symmetry's great mavens. His Nobel Prize was for showing that symmetry relations play a fundamental role in chemical reactions. My particular symmetry theory was less magnitudinous, but I thought he might enjoy it.

The idea came in a blinding moment of insight last fall [1998], the kind of epiphany that caused Archimedes to shout from his tub, "Give me a place to stand, and I will take a shower!" Symmetry was behind baseball's subtlety and complexity, I realized. Football and basketball, for example, have a simple spatial symmetry. The playing areas are bilaterally symmetrical, and the teams are of equal numbers. But in baseball, the symmetry is temporal: teams alternate their use of the same space. And symmetry is broken in the numbers of players—always nine on defense, anywhere from one to four at any time on offense. These conditions of symmetry, I argued to Hoffmann, give baseball its depth and texture. He listened patiently. Then he squinted slightly and threw me an exploding, knee-high slider. "But it's so slow," he said.

Hoffmann, as usual, happens to be correct. The game can be downright torpid at times. But the inactivity is punctuated by moments of blinding speed: balls may zoom to the plate at close to 100 miles per hour—and get batted back even faster. In the college game, baseballs have been returning to the mound so fast, in fact, that scientists have been called in to help protect pitchers from being hoisted on their own petards. (A baseball, by the way, exhibits D_{2d} point group symmetry, for you chemists keeping score at home.)

According to the National Collegiate Athletic Association (NCAA), as many as twenty college pitchers each season have to leave games because they are hurt badly enough by shots from aluminum and other almost unbreakable, non-wood bats. The NCAA, therefore, announced last year that it wants to impose a speed limit on the belt-high way between batter and pitcher. The moundsmen will still be able to fling the ball to the plate as fast as they can, but the batters will not be allowed to hit the ball with an initial velocity exceeding 93 miles per hour.

Of course, asking hitters to ease up would be contrary to every healthy American's competitive instincts. No guidelines will deny any individual batsman the right to swing as hard as he wants. The laws of physics are being trusted to slow the ball down, as new bat specifications now being tested should impose the NCAA's will. A batter may still hit a fly, but he wouldn't hurt one.

Although maximum diameters and relations between length and mass come into play, the bottom line is straightforward: heavier bats. Obviously, players cannot uncoil cumbersome clubs quite as quickly. The drop in swing speed translates to slower slaps back to the mound. That in turn means that student-athletes won't have their brains scrambled by anything other than deciphering why Hoffmann has suggested that the *endo* preference in Diels-Alder reactions is a secondary effect of orbital symmetry.

One other launched projectile note: just a Mark McGwire moonshot away from Yankee Stadium sits the Bronx Zoo, home to Tunuka, a gorilla pegged by the *New York Daily News* as the "primate suspect" in a 1995 rock-throwing incident in which an eight-year-old boy was allegedly beaned.

The boy's family is now suing the zoo for a million bananas. The *News* story was written by someone actually named FitzGibbon. I have yet to figure out all the symmetry rules in play here, but I'm working on it.

GREAT FEETS

WALKING ON WATER TAKES A MAN WITH MIGHTY BIG SHOES TO FILL

June 2000

Fish gotta swim. Birds gotta fly. What doesn't gotta happen is what an Alsatian man named Rémy Bricka likes to do— walk on water. In March, Bricka began what he hoped would be a walk, on buoyant ski-length footgear, across the Pacific Ocean. Because it is there, presumably.

Bricka already holds a place in the *Guinness Book of Records* by virtue of a previous tromp across the Atlantic in 1988. Normal journalistic practice would include an attempt to reach Bricka for a first-person account. That idea ground to a halt upon contemplation of the words of linguistic philosopher Ludwig Wittgenstein: "If a lion could talk, we would not understand it." Just as the uniquely leonine experience imposes a worldview that would make meaningful communication impossible, the Bricka experience probably placed him beyond my comprehension. My father really is a carpenter who really is named Joseph, but any messiah complex I may have is too puny to help me figure out why somebody wants to walk on water. And I haven't even mentioned that Bricka takes leave from his job as a one-man band to take his walks.

Actually, lots of guys walk on water all the time. They are called hockey players. But restricting the discussion to water in the liquid phase, your average human makes a poor pond pedestrian. Bricka's passion, however, made me wonder about the creatures—none great, all small—that truly can keep their feet above water.

Such animals exploit various physical principles to stay afloat. Robert B. Suter, a biologist at Vassar College, studies one such critter, the aptly named fishing spider. He explains that its legs produce tiny dimples on the water thanks to surface tension, the slight attraction of water molecules to one another that becomes a Brobdingnagian factor at Lilliputian scales. "What makes the dimple stay intact is surface tension, and a lot of the force that holds the spider up is surface tension," Suter says. Add the water's drag, and when the spider drives a leg against its dimple, voilà, it's walking.

Although there are characteristics of rowing involved here, and despite the fact that the dimples also act as hulls and impart an additional slight buoyancy, this process seems much like the kind of walking with which we humans are familiar. A leg pushes against a surface that pushes back. So while I hate to burst his bubble, Bricka's walks seem misclassified. He is actually a conventional sailor sailing unconventional vessels: two boats that happen to be on his feet.

On the other hand, Bricka could become a genuine water walker through modified gear that would allow surface tension to work its magic. He needs to get edgier, the edge in question being where water, air and foot meet and where surface tension does its stuff. Calculations, for freshwater, by Mark W. Denny of Stanford University show that a 110-pound person could walk on water using footwear with a total perimeter of about 6.7 kilometers. Laces surely sold separately. A bigger challenge than walking the Pacific would then be wearing both shoes at the same time.

An alternative noted by Steven Vogel of Duke University is severe weight reduction. Assuming Bricka wears about a size 9, his feet alone would support him on the water if he managed to slim down to about five grams, an accomplishment that would render the ensuing Pacific walk a mere footnote.

All this advice comes too late. Bricka's march on the sea, which he had estimated would take six months, was over almost before he could wave good-bye. On day one, a storm wrecked the catamaran he towed behind him, costing him food, supplies and bed. And so his mare trek came to an end. Fortunately, he escaped unscathed and continues to walk among us. Because he didn't sink. Like a bricka.

NUMBER ONE

THANKS TO THIS WOMAN, YOU CAN READ IT IN THE PAPER

December 2004

When my plane landed at the Akron-Canton airport in Ohio this past October, I was thinking about urine. True, I drank two cups of coffee before the hour-long flight from New York City. But I was thinking about urine because during the trip I read an Associated Press article about industry attempts to create synthetic urine. The idea of artificially making something that exists naturally in an endless stream might appear to be as silly as, oh, I don't know, cloning sheep. But there is actually a role for synthetic urine as a standard for calibrating equipment used in urine tests. Yes, there's a market for faux pee. Little did I know that the next day I would meet a woman who made her mark with the real thing.

I was in Akron to attend the Collegiate Inventors Competition awards ceremony at the National Inventors Hall of Fame. Numerous members of that institution also showed up. And that's how I met chemist Helen Free, a hall of famer, former president of the American Chemical Society and a monarch of micturition: Free is affectionately known as the Pee Queen. Helen and her late husband, colleague and fellow hall of famer Alfred Free, invented the strips of paper that can simply be dipped in a urine sample and then matched against a color code to indicate the levels of various substances. (Coincidentally, a few miles from the Inventors Hall of Fame is the Pro Football Hall of Fame, another institution whose members are intimately acquainted with urine testing.)

In the early 1950s, Helen told me, she and Alfred worked together in the diagnostics division at Miles Laboratories in Elkhart, Ind. With diabetes then, as now, one of the country's major health problems, the Frees were trying to come up with an easy way for diabetics to test for glucose in urine at home. They had the idea of permeating paper with several chemicals that were sensitive to the presence of glucose.

A few drops of urine on the paper would cause a color change if the urine contained any glucose. "And then," Helen remembers, "Al, bless his heart, said, 'What would happen if you impregnated the reagents in the paper and then just dipped it in the urine, like a litmus test?' And that became Clinistix, the first dip-and-read test of any kind." Dip-and-read strips have since been developed that test urine for numerous other medically important compounds.

During the research phase of their easy glucose test, the Frees reversed the usual tradition of reminding children to flush. Their six kids were put to work as a urine production facility. And all that valuable urine needed to be stored. Helen says a caveat in the Free household thus was, "Beware of anything yellow in the refrigerator. It may not be Mountain Dew."

Always active in science education, Helen Free was once demonstrating dip-and-read strips to a group of other people's children when she discovered that a scientist can never assume anything as a given. The particular test was for occult blood. "These little kids, with their noses right about at the same height as the demonstration table, stopped by and said, 'What ya got?' And we were telling them that this urine has blood and that one doesn't, and you dip the strips and see which one turns blue. And at the end we said, 'Do you have any questions?' And one of them said, 'Yeah. What's urine?'"

There are no stupid questions, though, which gives me the courage to modify an old axiom to ask: Would I rather have a Free bottle in front of me than a prefrontal lobotomy?

ALCOHOL, TOBACCO, AND SOY ALARMS

ANALYSIS OF LARGE NUMBERS OF PEOPLE CAN TURN UP SOME SURPRISING INSIGHTS ABOUT THE THINGS WE PUT IN OUR MOUTHS

July 2000

Epidemiologists are the unsung heroes of medicine. Emergency room physicians and their co-workers garner the good press and get entire television series devoted to their exploits. The attention is richly deserved, because they perform truly gallant labors. But the hard fact is that the ER docs save lives one at a time. Epidemiologists, through their analyses of the health and habits of big groups of people, save lives wholesale.

The other hard facts are (a) a TV show about epidemiologists would be about as exciting as vanilla ice cream, not to mention that this particular vanilla ice cream wouldn't get eaten because of epidemiological studies showing the dangers of high-fat diets, and (b) epidemiologists drive us crazy. Is margarine better than butter? This week, possibly; tune in next week for the latest exciting findings.

This past April saw a small shower of epidemiological publications that made the eyes glaze and the head spin, which anecdotal evidence associates with dizziness or demonic possession.

Item: Tofu or not tofu? The bland bastion of vegetarianism, tofu got its first bad press outside of a restaurant review. A study in the April issue of the *Journal of the American College of Nutrition* noted a connection between tofu consumption during middle age with cognitive impairment in later years. The data lead to the chilling conclusion that eating lots of tofu is correlated with losing the equivalent of three years of education. In other words, if you ate tofu twice a week all through junior high school you were just about breaking even. Can't recall who wrote the *Federalist Papers?* Maybe tofu's to blame. Think that Calculus is the hero of the movie *Gladiator?* Tofu may be the culprit. Not sure what the heck tofu is? Might be the tofu. (Decreased rates of cancer and heart disease? Also might be the tofu.)

Item: Cigarettes fail to fend off the tofu effect. A few small studies had intimated that smoking might protect against Alzheimer's disease and other forms of dementia, probably thanks to the nicotine. But research involving more than 34,000 men, published in the April 22 issue of the *British Med-*

ical Journal, found no brain-preserving effect from cigarettes. The *BMJ* paper thus grabs medicinal smokers by the lapels and says, "Wise up." (The authors include Richard Doll and Richard Peto—these guys are just about the most famous epidemiologists out there, if such a description isn't oxymoronic.)

Item: Beer is really good for you, so maybe they can sell it in the part of the health food store formerly reserved for tofu. Red wine gets most of the health praise reserved for adult beverages, but a study in the April 29 issue of the *Lancet* finds that beer may be even better. All alcohol raises levels of homocysteine, and that's bad, as homocysteine is associated with heart disease and counters some of alcohol's good intentions. But beer also includes pyridoxine, and that's good, because it keeps homocysteine levels down. Pyridoxine is more commonly known as vitamin B_6, which will henceforth be less commonly known as B_6-pack.

Item: Beer is really bad for you, in ways you probably couldn't imagine. A study in the April 28 issue of the *Morbidity and Mortality Weekly Report,* published by the Centers for Disease Control and Prevention, concludes that cheap beer leads to gonorrhea. The relation presumably results from the powers of beer to get young adults to engage in risky behaviors, such as driving or other things you can do in a car. The authors estimate that a twenty-cent tax hike per six-pack should lower national rates of gonorrhea by almost 9 percent, apparently by forcing some people to keep their hands in their own, empty pockets.

In conclusion, then, epidemiological studies prove that smoking totally stinks and that the old adage should now read: Eat (but be careful of tofu despite its many other probable health benefits), drink (but make it a beer and please be willing to pay a little more for it for the benefit of society as a whole), and be merry. Which has no downside. Yet.

UNCOMMON SCENTS

A WHIFF AT THE PLATE BRINGS UP A BOUQUET OF POSSIBILITIES

November 2006

New York Yankee great Derek Jeter usually comes up smelling like a rose. But according to mid-August news reports, Jeter will soon also smell like "chilled grapefruit, clean oakmoss and spice." Those odors are the elements of the shortstop's new men's perfume—I mean cologne—to be sold under the name Driven. (It's the scent that says, "I'm not stopping at second base.")

Athletes thus join movie stars and other celebrities in having their own signature fragrances, for sale to the malodorous masses. But, although scientists are vital to the fragrance industry, there are no fragrances honoring them. So here are some suggestions for a new line of scientist-inspired scents.

Isaac Newton's *Gravitas*
Ingredients: Fresh-cut grass, royal mint and, of course, apple spice.
Slogan: For the man who likes his heavenly bodies as far away as possible.

J. Robert Oppenheimer's *Cataclysm*
Ingredients: Desert sand, enriched geranium.
Slogan: Now I am become Death, the destroyer of worlds, but with a delicate floral hint.

Barbara McClintock's *Transposition*
Ingredients: Corn kernels, corn husk, Cornell.
Slogan: When your genes make that unexpected move.

Alan Turing's *Enigma*
Ingredients: Sptf qfubmt.
Slogan: Tell them it's the real you.

Nikola Tesla's *Genius*
Ingredients: Secret.
Slogan: Change the world.
(Note: Removed from market; formula lost.)

Alessandro Volta's *Charge*
Ingredients: Cat hair, amber, balloons.
Slogan: Make sparks fly.

Antoine Lavoisier's *Chemistry*
Ingredients: Hydrogen, oxygen.
Slogan: When the elements come together, you may lose your head.

Ludwig Wittgenstein's *Logic*
Ingredient: Silence.

Slogan: For when you don't have the words to say the things you mean.

Anton van Leeuwenhoek's *Hidden*
Ingredient: Pond water.
Slogan: Reveal . . . the little things.

Socrates' *Philosophy*
Ingredients: Olive oil, feta cheese, traces of hemlock.
Slogan: You fill me with . . . questions.

Albert Einstein's *Continuum*
(undoubtedly to be renamed *Relativity* after disappointing early sales)
Ingredient: Thyme.
Slogan: The faster you go, the shorter you get.

Stephen Hawking's *Universe*
Ingredients: Everything.
Slogan: You don't have to understand it.

Michael Faraday's *Dynamo*
Ingredients: Copper, mercury, rubber.
Slogan: Your magnetism will create . . . electricity.

Kurt Gödel's *Theorem*
Ingredients: Complete list unavailable.
Slogan: For the man who has almost everything.

Galileo Galilei's *Insight*
Ingredient: Patronage.
Slogan: Discover new worlds.

Benjamin Franklin's *Revolution*
Ingredient: Sage.
Slogan: Come in from the rain.

Stephen Jay Gould's *Evolution*
Ingredients: Flamingo smiles, hen's teeth, panda thumbs.
Slogan: Punctuate your equilibrium.

Leonardo da Vinci's *Invention*
Ingredients (written backward on label): Oil-based pigment.
Slogan: Leave a lady smiling.

IT'S NOT OEUVRE TILL IT'S OEUVRE

October 1999

You can observe a lot just by watching, according to one of the foremost neurolinguists of our time, Lawrence Peter Berra, known as Yogi to his many disciples. If you've been watching the news, you may have observed the music of Mozart getting a lot of attention in recent years as a brain enhancer. For more than half a century, Yogi has endured ballpark organs playing the decidedly non-Mozartian ditty, "ta ta ta TA ta TAAAA," which implores the fans to then scream "charge." But because Yogi also wondered, "How can you think and hit at the same time?" he probably didn't cry foul at the lack of any brain-building melodies emanating from stadium loudspeakers.

Turns out he probably wasn't missing anything (especially high fastballs). A study in the July 1999 issue of the journal *Psychological Science*, from Kenneth Steele and his colleagues at Appalachian State University, disputes those isolated previous findings indicating that a few minutes of Mozart, specifically the Sonata for Two Pianos (K. 448), raise the spatial reasoning capacity of test subjects, albeit temporarily. The attention paid to the so-called Mozart effect helped to pave the way for some pregnant women to slap headphones on their swelled bellies, so that the symphonic could mix with the amniotic to induce the mnemonic and other brainy stuff. Additional histrionics could be found in Georgia, where all new mothers now get classical CDs as a public health measure.

Now, I admire Mozart as much as the next guy, especially if the next guy is Salieri. (I've even had the privilege of playing some Mozart—K. 622, for you fans keeping a score at home.) But those earlier studies, even had they been verified, were still quite limited. They only looked at that one Mozart composition and only compared its effects to silence and to a work by the minimalist composer Philip Glass, who sometimes puts me into a lovely trance state and sometimes makes me seek out the hardest flat surface I can find so I may, rhythmically and repeatedly, bang my head. So, bottom line, listening to Mozart proba-bly doesn't make you smart. In fact, it's usually the other way around.

In other news showing that a little data may go a long way, the American Academy of Pediatrics issued a report in August recommending that children under the age of two be shielded from the corrosive effects of television by being totally prohibited from watching it. (The new Mozart study does away with the awkward conflicts that would have been posed by televised productions of *Don Giovanni*.) The lead author of the report admitted that hardly anything is known about TV's effect on kids two and under. But she jus-tified the ban by noting that the known requirements for proper brain development—you get smart from a bonanza of good times with all in the family—have less of a chance of happening if the baby's butt is parked in front of the tube all day. She's probably right, although it would be ironic if thirty years from now research were to show that the adults best able to function in a world where most commu-nication of information is taking place on video screens were precisely those who learned to program the VCR be-fore they could walk to the mailbox to get the *TV Guide*.

So what's a parent to do? Keeping a child away from un-healthy influences is an obvious and heartfelt desire. On the other hand, Mom eventually has to do the laundry. (I'm not being sexist—we all know that it's Mom who does the laundry.) If Barney keeps the little guy happy for the time needed to hang up the fine washables, will Mom disregard the pediatricians' recommendation? The contemplation of this kind of tough decision is what led Yogi to perhaps his most Zen-like revelation: "If you come to a fork in the road, take it." Now there's a thought that indicates some serious spatial reasoning capacity.

MEMBERS ONLY

A LOOK AT SOME RECENT RESEARCH THAT COULD BE DESCRIBED AS ORGANIC

December 2002

It happens this way sometimes. Just as Leibniz and Newton independently invented the calculus, certain scientific advances just seem to be in the air. Throw in the fact that most scientists are male, and perhaps it begins to explain why you couldn't swing Schrödinger's cat in September 2002 without hitting breaking news about penises.

First came a report in the *Journal of Urology* that scientists at Harvard Medical School had successfully grown rabbit penis parts in petri plates (which Peter Piper particularly appreciated), a first step toward growing whole penises. My initial reaction was, "Do we really need the ratio of rabbit penises to male rabbits to be greater than one?"

The researchers removed sections of rabbits' penises, took some of the harvested cells, and grew lots of new ones from them, then implanted the freshly grown tissue back in the donor rabbits. The restored rabbits appeared to function fine, although they probably took to walking gingerly rather than hopping down the bunny trail. Of course, the aim of this work is to eventually be able to create human tissue for men in need of reconstructive surgery because of disease or injury. But the technology could also someday benefit otherwise healthy guys who decided *not* to spend the money on the Lamborghini.

Next came the news from a meeting of the British Association for the Advancement of Science of the discovery of the world's oldest fossilized penis. The member belonged to a crustacean from Brazil (where the nuts come from) that frolicked some 100 million years ago. Now, it wasn't a big piece of machinery, as the entire organism was only about a millimeter long. But the penis took up about one third of the little guy's body length and volume. Extinction, perhaps, was inevitable.

Then came a Reuters report that Levi Strauss & Co. was coming out with a new kind of Dockers pants that, like some other pants, includes a special pocket for your cell phone. Only the pocket of the so-called Icon S-Fit (emphasis on the "con") includes a "radiation-reducing" lining, presumably to protect a man's private parts from the signals sent and received by cell phones. "We're not implying in any way that cell phones are dangerous," said a Levi spokesman whose name really is Cedric Jungpeter or I wouldn't be able to say it was.

Jungpeter also said, "Our intention is not to cash in on consumer fears but provide the consumers with what they want." And if the company happens to cash in on consumer fears despite that not being their intention, well, hey. By the way, I have a question: If the pocket successfully blocks radiation, how can calls get through? And if calls can't get through anyway, why not just shut the phone off before putting it in your pocket?

A shoe story came on the heels of the pants story (which has to be the most confused metaphor in this issue). New research, in the *British Journal of Urology International*, established the relation between shoe size and . . . sock size. In fact, the study dispelled the commonly held belief that shoe size is an indicator of penis size. Two London urologists enlisted 104 men for the study. The urologists write, "The linear distance from the symphysis pubis to the tip of the glans along the dorsal aspect, under maximal extension of the phallus, was recorded using a measuring tape," which translates to "we somehow got 104 guys to agree to drop their pants next to a tape rule."

They then compared the numbers with shoe size data and found no correlation. One of the urologists, clearly frustrated by the nonfinding, was quoted by Reuters Health news service as saying, "There must be some part of the body that is predictive of penile length. . . . The search continues." In the future, of course, penis size will be highly correlated with petri dish size.

DOWN IN FRONT

November 1999

James Madison was a pivotal player in American history, one of the giants who created this country. He co-wrote the *Federalist Papers*. He was the key figure in the writing and ratification of the Constitution. After a stint as Thomas Jefferson's secretary of state, he became the fourth president of the U.S. *Boy, could we use a guy like that today*, you may be thinking. Except that today Madison would probably have to take a tour to get into the White House, as Americans no longer elect presidents who need help reaching their cabinet's top shelf. At five feet four inches, Madison was, in the words of Washington Irving, "a withered little apple-John."

Now it turns out that Madison, in addition to being a political visionary, may have been physically ahead of his time too. Some downsizing, to Madisonian proportions or even less, may be in order. That's the thinking of Thomas Samaras, an engineer and systems analyst in the medium-size city of San Diego. For twenty-five years Samaras, at five feet ten inches, has been on a mission to convince people that Randy Newman was woefully small-minded when he sang, "Short people got no reason to live." According to Samaras, a world of people fit for the titles of Louisa May Alcott novels would not only live longer but would also be more environmentally friendly at the same time.

Samaras's conclusions are based on his entropy theory of aging. From a thermodynamic viewpoint, it holds that bigger people, being more energetic systems overall than smaller fry, are more likely to suffer from entropic increases in disorder that translate to disease and death. His most recent paper, in the Swedish pediatrics journal *Acta Paediatrica*, spells out some of the advantages the human race could enjoy if "short, dark, and handsome" became the ideal.

A long-lived short life seems to be one benefit. Numerous studies indicate that healthy small people outlive their larger counterparts. Samaras points out that a six-foot-tall man has about 100 trillion cells, whereas a five-footer has only about sixty trillion. "The tall man has forty trillion more potential sites for cancer to be initiated from free radicals, cosmic rays, high-energy photons, or mutagens from the air, food, and water," he and his co-authors write. All else being proportional, tall people's hearts have to work harder, pumping blood farther. And most damning to the lanky is the contention that "when a 20 percent taller person trips, he or she hits the ground with 210 percent more kinetic energy than a shorter person." This calculation is thus the first quantitative statement I've ever seen in a scientific journal for exactly how much harder they fall the bigger they come.

Samaras goes on to compare two hypothetical U.S. populations that differ in height by 10 percent. The big lugs would need some eighty million more acres of farmland just to feed themselves. They would also produce an extra, large mountain of garbage, some thirty-six million additional tons annually. Small people are just more efficient.

The same high-calorie, high-fat diets that promote chronic disease are also probably at least partly behind the rise in height (about an inch every generation this century) in the U.S. One key to reversing the trend toward superfluous height would be a nutritious diet, starting in childhood, that did not promote the kind of showy bigness that saunters down fashion show runways. The average person then eventually might be six to eight inches less inelegantly tall than are today's big shots.

Will humanity get down? Cultural imperatives will probably prevent it in the short term. For now, Samaras makes do with his recommendation for "scientists and medical professionals to educate their patients, students and the public about the advantages of shorter human size." His quest seems to have a worthwhile objective. The best views are achieved not by virtue of height but by standing on the shoulders of Madisons.

TELEVISION COVERAGE

A MODEST PROPOSAL FOR SMALL SCREENING IN MEDICINE

May 2004

In January 2004, a Romanian woman underwent surgery in a Bucharest hospital to remove a 175-pound tumor. News reports quoted a plastic surgeon at the hospital as having delivered the startling revelation that "the lack of the tumor really suits her."

Of course, 175-pound tumors don't grow overnight. And the woman had apparently tried for years to raise money for the operation. The Discovery Channel finally forked over the funding, in exchange for film rights.

Finding money for medical treatment can also be a problem in the U.S. This past February saw the release of the *Economic Report of the President*, which noted that more than forty-three million people in this country lack health insurance. The report also stressed that "U.S. markets provide incentives to develop innovative health care products and services that benefit both Americans and the global community."

Keeping those sentiments and the Romanian tumor case in mind, one solution becomes obvious. Uninsured patients, who have not appreciated that their diseases are in fact valuable market commodities, could sell their conditions to television programs, which would pay for medical treatment.

In that spirit, here are some suggestions for the fall lineup of new series:

NEW PROGRAMS GUIDE

Everybody Loves Radiology. A dysfunctional family is crammed into a magnetic resonance imager to see who can stay in the longest. The last one left gets scanned and treated if the MRI finds anything funny.

American Eye Doc. Glaucoma patients do cost-benefit analyses of getting their meds either through pharmacies or from a guy called Spliffy the Bongmeister.

E.R.R. An attorney has complete access to a public hospital's medical records for one hour to find the best malpractice case. The patient, if living, then gets to choose: sue, settle, or a "do-over" at a private hospital.

Just Don't Shoot Me. Twelve unrestrained four-year-olds are put into a room with a pediatrician who has eleven doses of DTP vaccine.

The Simple Life-Threatening Emergency. A full checkup is the prize as uninsured contestants attempt to use the Heimlich maneuver to dislodge a foreign object from Paris Hilton.

Let's Make a Drug Deal. The audience watches as a patient with multiple preexisting conditions gets to choose pharmaceutical treatment for only one.

American Choppers. A panel of judges rates octogenarians as they eat corn on the cob and bob for apples, with the winner receiving a full set of new dentures.

Barely Live with Regis and Kelly. One lucky audience member gets medical care—if he or she is sitting in the seat with the same number as the one chosen at random by a caller.

N.Y.P.D. Code Blue. A police car has thirty minutes to get a patient with chest pains from Manhattan's Lower East Side to the Upper West Side, with treatment guaranteed if they make it. Warning: May contain nude images of Dennis Franz, which should be viewed only by contestants from American Eye Doc.

Dr. Timothy Johnson's Jackass. Johnson, the ABC News medical editor, personally treats kids injured jumping off their roofs, riding shopping carts down hills or imitating pro wrestlers.

CSI: Bethesda. An uninsured elite forensics team tries to determine how a private pharmaceutical company got a proprietary interest in a product created through publicly funded research at the National Institutes of Health.

The Price Is Nuts. People who actually have insurance but still can't afford their 50 percent co-pay on mental health care try to guess the cost of an hour-long session with their nearest competent therapist without going over.

Parasite Island. Six eighteen- to thirty-four-year-olds dine at an all-you-can-eat discount sushi bar and then evaluate the proposition in the *Economic Report of the President* that some young people "may remain uninsured because they are young and healthy and do not see the need for insurance."

THIS IS ONLY A TEST

February 1999

Because the vast majority of our readers have some experience with being in high school, we now pay homage to that great tradition that brought sweat to the palms of so many: the pop quiz. If you are one of those amazing devotees of the magazine who know its pages inside and out, the following should be fun for you. If you're a more casual reader, you will still have a good time. And if you picked up this issue by accident at a newsstand, buy it and leave it on your coffee table to impress people. (Television star Paul Reiser did it in an episode of *Mad about You*. I do it too, only I don't have to buy it. *[Editors' note: He does now.]* Anyway, the true/false trivia questions that follow are based on material that appeared in *Scientific American* in 1998.

1. We proudly made it through all of 1998 without once publishing the word "Lewinsky."

Regrettably, this is *false*. (And now we've blown 1999 too.) The word "Lewinsky" appears in the November issue on page 110. So does a picture of Monica, in an article on the history of magnetic recording. Linda Tripp, however, is not pictured, nor does she appear in the August issue's article on lower back pain.

2. We published an article that discussed the work of a scientist who had a metal nose.

True. The article appears on page 116 of the July issue, and the noseless man in question is the great Danish astronomer Tycho Brahe. So how did he smell? Probably pretty bad: daily showers were still a few centuries off, and there was indeed something rotten in Denmark.

3. We printed a photograph of a team of horses pulling a boat.

True. The photograph appears on page 63 of the February issue, in an article on Viking longships. Horses were put to the task of pulling longships over short stretches of land between bodies of water.

4. We printed a photograph of a boat pulling a team of horses.

False. Unless you want to be a real stickler for Newton's third law. In that case, *true*, same picture.

5. We ran an X-ray image of a mosquito's knee.

True. The phase-contrast X-ray micrograph appears on page 73 of the December issue, in the article "Making Ultra-bright X-rays."

6. We ran an X-ray of a bee's knees.

False. The bee's knees? Hey, it's 1999; this magazine no longer employs such antiquated verbiage, although the column "50, 100, and 150 Years Ago" still features vestigial usage such as "twenty-three skidoo" and "Nobel prize for DDT." So, no, there were no bee's knees. In an article in the April issue on the images seen by early microscopists, however, we do publish a view of the head of a louse, on page 52. Another louse appears in the November issue on the bottom of page 107, standing in a car, sporting a silly little mustache and planning world domination.

Bonus essay question: Why only six questions?
We ran out of space for anything more.

Extra bonus: Why does this quiz on 1998 appear in February rather than January?

We accuse the Y2K bug, thereby laying claim to being the first to blame it for something that has actually happened.

CHAPTER 4

The Human Comedy

GOOD FELLOWS

HOLMES IS WHERE THE HEART IS, BUT HE DESERVES SOME COMPANY

January 2003

Truth is stranger than fiction, it is often said. Well, this is the truth—in October 2002 England's Royal Society of Chemistry granted an honorary fellowship to a fictional character who is no stranger: Sherlock Holmes. A spokesperson for the society was quoted as saying that the recognition was for Holmes's "love of chemistry, and the way that he wielded such knowledge for the public good, employing it dispassionately and analytically."

If any fabricated person deserves membership in a real science organization, Sherlock's surely a (gum)shoo-in. But don't other pretend people and assorted chimerical characters also merit fellowships in various real science societies? In the Holmesian spirit, here are a few nominations.

American Ornithologists' Union: The Road Runner, for research on the predator-prey relationship, specifically within the context of avian flightlessness.

American Institute of Physics: Wile E. Coyote, for his literally groundbreaking studies, performed in collaboration with the Road Runner, on falling objects and rapid deceleration.

International Society for Prosthetics and Orthotics: Captain Ahab, for overcoming adversity and maintaining a position of authority despite being differently abled.

American Society of Transplant Surgeons: Dr. Victor Frankenstein, for his innovative research on the art and science of multiple organ, limb, bone—well, pretty much everything—transplantation.

Academy of Criminal Justice Sciences: Jean Valjean, for his long-term study of recidivism and techniques involved in successful rehabilitation of convicted felons.

American Society for Adolescent Psychiatry: Holden Caulfield, for his studies of the American postwar adolescent experience.

American Board of Sport Psychology: Mighty Casey, for striking out and thus illustrating the pitfalls of unfounded high self-esteem, while at the same time bringing no joy to Mudville, thereby illustrating the dangers of investment in external sources of gratification.

Society for Endocrinology: Paul Bunyan, for actualizing his personal experience, despite an obvious and potentially debilitating endocrine disorder. (Note: The Sierra Club may protest this citation.)

International Society of Entomology: Gregor Samsa, for his serendipitous study of the social life of the common cockroach.

The International Association for Research in Economic Psychology and the American Society of Agronomy, jointly: Willy Loman, for his enduring efforts to educate others about the importance of being well liked for success in sales and marketing and for his forceful hypothesis that a man is not a piece of fruit.

American Association for Marriage and Family Therapy: Anna Karenina, for identifying individualized unhappiness within the family unit.

American Association of Amateur Astronomers: Popeye, for the countless new stars and other celestial objects he discovered—thanks to his spinach-enhanced punches—orbiting Bluto's head.

American Meteorological Society and National Geographic Society, jointly: Dorothy Gale, for employing tornadoes in the discovery of new lands and peoples.

American Heart Association: The Scarecrow, for his tenacious efforts to obtain a heart despite his apparent capacity to get along without one.

American Society of Metallurgists: Rumplestiltskin, for his imaginative insights in the field of transmutation, specifically involving the conversion of common base material into precious metal.

American Podiatric Medical Association: Achilles, for his elucidation of the vital importance of foot health care.

Linguistic Society of America: Presidents Josiah Bartlet (*The West Wing*), Tom Beck (*Deep Impact*), Andrew Shepherd (*The American President*) and James Marshall (*Air Force One*), for their ability to construct complete, grammatically coherent sentences.

And, finally:

Royal Agricultural Society of England: Dr. John Watson, for being the quintessential second banana (and thereby offering evidence disputing the theoretical agronomy of Willy Loman).

Author's note: See next essay for further comment about the Heartless Scarecrow.

THE RAEL THING

IT'S NOT A MEDIA CIRCUS WITHOUT THE CLONE CAR

March 2003

By the time you read this, one of four things has happened: (1) Someone has presented conclusive evidence that a newborn baby was, in fact, cloned from an adult. I would sooner bet that the next time you watch *The Wizard of Oz* the flying monkeys are replaced by flying pigs. (2) Someone is claiming that a newborn baby, who at least has been identified and photographed, is a clone. Someone may very well claim it, but I'm going double or nothing on the flying pigs. (3) Those touting their mystery clone babies as I am writing these words in mid-January will have stopped holding news conferences. (4) They're still holding news conferences, but reporters have stopped showing up for them, presumably to cover the flying pig story.

The Raelians' assertions of successful clone concoction were so widely covered in late December and early January that I need not review the details here. But a couple of points are worth mentioning. First, kudos to Donald G. McNeil, Jr., whose coverage of the Raelian misconception for the *New York Times* included the following: "Raelians are followers of Rael, a French-born former race-car driver who has said he met a four-foot space alien atop a volcano in southern France in 1973 and went aboard his ship, where he was entertained by voluptuous female robots and learned that the first humans were created 25,000 years ago by space travelers called Elohim, who cloned themselves." It's not clear whether the alien was green, but I am, with envy—I'll never write anything that funny.

Second, special thanks to Michael Guillen, a physicist turned freelance TV journalist, for his tireless work "on behalf of the world's press," as he put it. What Guillen was prepared to do, at what he said was the Raelians' invitation, was organize and oversee a panel of scientific experts that would determine the veracity of the clone's heredity. A physicist is especially useful in dealing with cloning questions: for example, using a sensitive enough barometer, a physicist could measure the atmospheric pressure at the top of a standing baby clone's head and at the soles of its feet and tell you the exact height of that baby clone. (If a clone's foot even *has* a sole.)

Unfortunately, or maybe fortunately, the Raelians quickly withdrew their offer to actually produce the baby, so to speak, citing the privacy concerns of the parents. I'm not sure how many parents a clone has, although I'd guess the number is an integer equal to or greater than zero. But I could be wrong.

Speaking of both being wrong and the aforementioned *Wizard of Oz*, many thanks to the numerous readers who e-mailed to tell me that, like the Scarecrow, I lack a brain. Why else, while nominating fictional characters for membership in real scientificorganizations two issues ago, would I have written that the Scarecrow belonged in the American Heart Association for his efforts to procure a heart? [See Good Fellows, page 153.]

T. Richard Halberstadt of Wyoming, Ohio (make up your mind, T.), noted that his "four-year-old granddaughter, who dresses herself in red shoes and a blue-and-white-checked dress as often as her mother will let her, could tell you that it is the Tin Woodman, not the Scarecrow, who wanted a heart." Many fellow staffers have told me that I, too, have the mind of a four-year-old, who was glad to get rid of it.

J. Quinn Brisben (a real person, not a Groucho Marx character) of Chicago noted my error and then faintly praised, "Not everyone can be Martin Gardner or Douglas Hofstadter [two former *Scientific American* writers], and you are doing tolerably well." All I can say to that is, I know I have a heart, because it's breaking.

THE YANKED CLIPPERS

HAVE SOME SECURITY MEASURES BECOME MORONIC, OR IS IT JUST ME?

July 2003

It was my nagging fear of inadvertently carrying nail clippers while trying to pass through airport security, as well as my long-standing interest in stupidity, that prompted me to go hear Simon Davies present the first Stupid Security Awards at the Conference on Computers, Freedom, and Privacy in April 2003 here in New York City. Davies, director of Privacy International, a nonprofit organization based in London and Washington, D.C., went through almost 5,000 nominations from people telling tales of unnecessary intrusion and harassment in the service of the *illusion* of security—I mean, seriously, can't sharp fingernails be as lethal as a set of nail clippers?

I also went because overzealous and counterproductive security is a science issue. In December 2002 the presidents of the National Academy of Sciences, the National Academy of Engineering and the Institute of Medicine issued a joint statement complaining that "outstanding young scientists, engineers, and health researchers have been prevented from or delayed in entering this country."

In February an online article by Peg Brickley in the *Scientist Daily News* pointed out that visa delays had prevented the return of fifteen Cornell University students who had gone home for winter break, resulting in "research left half-done." Like it isn't already tough enough to get people to go to Ithaca in the middle of winter. (By mid-May most stranded students were back, but Cornell expected fresh problems in the next semester.)

In addition, the article outlined the case of two Bangladeshi physicians, one Hindu and one Muslim, who were being brought to Ithaca by Cornell researcher Kathleen Rasmussen through a training grant from the National Institutes of Health's Fogarty International Center, which "promotes and supports scientific research and training internationally to reduce disparities in global health," according to its mission statement. The Hindu physician had no difficulty. The Muslim's visa was repeatedly denied, finally approved but then ultimately left unprocessed. "From the point of view of someone trying to run a government grant to meet government purposes with government money," Rasmussen said, "to have the left and right hands working against each other is very disturbing." Her statement is quite true and also happens to explain the average person's aversion to accordion music.

The Stupid Security Awards, on the other other hand, dealt with more mundane examples of people being annoyed and inconvenienced by dubious security measures. (The kind, for instance, that we at *Scientific American* deal with: after September 11, our building installed high-tech turnstiles in the lobby. These turnstiles can be negotiated only by someone brandishing an electronic ID card or with the ability to jump over a metal bar about three feet off the floor.)

Oddly, the award citations that Davies read at the conference do not match those listed on the Privacy International Website (www.privacyinternational.org). Maybe some kind of Orwellian historical alteration took place. Nevertheless, I recommend visiting the site for one version of the list of winners and for links to dozens of nominations, two of which I'll recount.

My favorite tale of "whoa" came from an airline pilot with clipper issues of his own. "I am searched as rigorously as any passenger," he wrote. "I am forbidden to have any nail clippers." The pilot then noted that "once on board the aircraft, securely locked away on the flight deck, I have an ax behind me."

A close second was submitted by a guy whose story starts as he is about to board a plane in San Francisco. "The polite inspector informed me that he had to check my shoes for explosives. I dutifully removed them and handed them to him. He picked them up one by one and slammed them down on the floor with full force. Apparently, as they hadn't exploded, they were not dangerous, and he handed them back to me." Perhaps it's best to look on the bright side and simply applaud any public display of the scientific method.

MONUMENTAL ERROR

APPARENTLY, TO PARAPHRASE GERTRUDE STEIN, WHEN YOU COME HERE, THERE'S NO HERE HERE

August 2006

On May 31, 2006, the Department of Homeland Security announced their 2006 antiterrorism funding grants to U.S. cities.

The New York Hall of Science. The New York Academy of Sciences. The New York Academy of Medicine. Albert Einstein College of Medicine. Columbia University College of Physicians and Surgeons. Weill Medical College of Cornell University. Mount Sinai School of Medicine. New York University School of Medicine. State University of New York Downstate Medical Center College of Medicine.

New York City had its funding cut by 40 percent from last year.

Nobel laureate Eric Kandel. Nobel laureate Richard Axel. Nobel laureate Roderick MacKinnon. Nobel laureate Harold Varmus. Nobel laureate Paul Greengard. Nobel laureate Joshua Lederberg. Nobel laureate Rosalyn Yalow.

Homeland Security officials said that they determined the amount of each grant based on a formula.

Ellis Island. The Brooklyn Bridge. The Throgs Neck Bridge. Linda Evangelista's neck. The Triborough Bridge. The 59th Street Bridge. Paul Simon. The Verrazano-Narrows Bridge. The George Washington Bridge.

The formula counts the presence of "national monuments or icons." Homeland Security officials determined that New York City had no such national monuments or icons.

The Statue of Liberty. The angel statue in Central Park. Belvedere Castle in Central Park. Central Park. Prospect Park. Van Cortlandt Park. Park Avenue. "Don't even THINK about parking here." Opera in the Parks. The New York Philharmonic. Derek Jeter. Grand Central Terminal. The Museum of Modern Art. The American Museum of Natural History. The Metropolitan Museum of Art. The Metropolitan Opera. The Mets. The rest of the Yankees. The rest of Linda Evangelista. Yankee Stadium. Madison Square Garden. Oh, okay, the Knicks and Rangers. Okay, even Shea Stadium. Coney Island. The bull statue on Wall Street. Wall Street. The Prometheus statue at Rockefeller Center. The skating rink at Rockefeller Center. Rockefeller Center. The Rockefeller University. Columbia University. New York University. The City University of New York. The New School. The Cooper Union for Advancement of Science and Art. The American Academy of Dramatic Arts. The Bronx High School of Science. Scientific American. Stuyvesant High School. Brooklyn Technical High School. Hunter College High School. The Juilliard School. The Fiorello H. LaGuardia High School of Music & Art and Performing Arts. Lincoln Center. Carnegie Hall. The Ziegfeld. David Letterman. Kurt Vonnegut. Ground Zero.

Scientists also develop formulas.

LGA. JFK. The FDR. The IRT. The IND. The BMT. The U.N.

When a formula produces results that are obviously nonsense, scientists examine the data.

The Empire State Building.

Responding to a hurricane of criticism, Homeland Security Secretary Michael Chertoff explained that the Empire State Building was purposefully placed in the "large office building" category rather than the icon category because that designation helps to generate a higher risk score. Here's a flash for the folks gaming their own formula: the Empire State Building is a large office building *and* an icon.

The Chrysler Building. The Flatiron Building. The Woolworth Building. St. Patrick's Cathedral. The New York Botanical Garden. The Brooklyn Botanic Garden. The New York Aquarium. The Queens Zoo. The Prospect Park Zoo. The Central Park Zoo. The Bronx Zoo.

When a formula produces results that are obviously nonsense, scientists may also scrutinize, modify, or even discard the formula itself. It's not easy, but somebody has to do it. Seriously, somebody *has* to.

COPY THAT

TECHNOLOGY IS MAKING IT HARDER FOR WORD THIEVES TO EARN OUTRAGEOUS FORTUNES

April 2002

It was the best of times, it was the worst of times,[1] it was the *New York Times*. Specifically, it was a *Times* article that discussed computer programs and other techniques designed to root out plagiarism.[2] The article revealed that there is now software that can look for a lengthy passage, like a string of pearls,[3] in a new document that is identical to a passage in a previously published work. In another method, every fifth word from sample passages is removed, and the author has to fill in the blanks[4] to reveal his or her familiarity with the work. These high-tech ways to spot literary theft will surely rob copycats of the sleep that knits up the raveled sleave of care.[5]

When I first read the *Times* article, I remember thinking, it's a good thing[6] and attention must be paid.[7] After all, as a writer, I find plagiarism to be a constant concern. (Although from time to time, I have to admit, I shall consider it.[8]) Of course, it can be hard to define. When you steal from one author, it's plagiarism; if you steal from many, it's research.[9] One might say that a writer should neither a borrower nor a lender be.[10] On the other hand, imitation is the sincerest form of flattery.[11]

I shall never believe that God plays dice with the world.[12] Therefore, the plagiarized passages that programs pinpoint are probably purposeful and potentially punishable.[13] There is grandeur in this view of life.[14] I think.[15]

Plagiarism is a central issue of science[16] as well. Relying on the work of others is the lifeblood of scientific research. Indeed, if I (who had the chance to learn physics that Newton never dreamed of) have seen further it is by standing on the shoulders of giants.[17] One might even say that I have always depended on the kindness of strangers[18] in this regard.

But employing the findings of other researchers is one thing; claiming such findings as one's own is intellectual murder most foul.[19] So when in the course of human events,[20] a case of plagiarism is revealed, it represents a clear and present danger[21] to intellectual liberty. And naturally, eternal vigilance is the price of liberty.[22] It is thus incumbent on all researchers to say, "Let me make this perfectly clear:[23] I am not a crook.[24]"

1   Dickens, Charles. *A Tale of Two Cities,* opening lines.
2   See Eakin, Emily. "Stop, Historians! Don't Copy That Passage! Computers Are Watching!" in the *New York Times,* January 26, 2002.
3   Miller, Glenn. Song title.
4   Rayburn, Gene. *The Match Game,* television program (1962–1969, 1973–1984).
5   Shakespeare, William. *Macbeth,* Act 2, Scene 2.
6   Stewart, Martha.
7   Miller, Arthur. *Death of a Salesman,* end of Act 1.
8   Spock, Mr. (with beard), to Captain Kirk on the transporter pad. *Star Trek,* episode 39, "Mirror, Mirror."
9   Mizner, Wilson (1876–1933).
10 Shakespeare, William. *Hamlet,* Act 1, Scene 3.
11 Colton, Charles Caleb (1780–1832).
12 Einstein, Albert, according to *Bartlett's Familiar Quotations.*
13 See Piper, Peter.
14 Darwin, Charles. *On the Origin of Species*, closing paragraph.
15 Descartes, René. "Cogito ergo sum."
16 "Science" refers to the enterprise by which human beings attempt to discover basic truths about the universe. It is, however, also the name of a journal published by the American Association for the Advancement of Science.
17 Attributed to Isaac Newton but probably existed in some form earlier.
18 Williams, Tennessee. *A Streetcar Named Desire,* 11.
19 Shakespeare, William. *Hamlet,* Act 1, Scene 5.
20 Declaration of Independence, opening paragraph.

21 Holmes, Oliver Wendell, Supreme Court justice. *Schenck v. United States,* 1919.

22 Phillips, Wendell (1811–1884). 1852 speech to the Massachusetts Antislavery Society, paraphrasing John Philpot Curran, who in 1790 said, "The condition upon which God hath given liberty to man is eternal vigilance."

23 Nixon, Richard M., thirty-seventh president of the United States. On numerous occasions.

24 Ibid., about the Watergate scandal.

DRAWING TO AN INSIDE FLUSH

A TALE OF TWO TOILETS

October 2006

In early August 2006, a short item crossed my desk about troubles on a movie set in Mumbai, formerly known as Bombay. Actors and crew were trying to film a scene in a public restroom for the Bollywood blockbuster *Keep at It, Munnabhai.* But when the actors walked past the autoflush urinals, they inadvertently set off the sensors. The water would noisily flow, and the scene would go down the drain. "At one point, with so many unit members inside the loo, all the flush sensors went berserk and started flushing simultaneously," recounted Raju Hirani, the film's director, according to the Associated Press. "We actually had to vacate the loo briefly to stop the urinals from flushing."

The flushing toilets of Mumbai (officially ranked as the 14,287th Wonder of the World, by the way, just behind the

Hanging Gardens of Piscataway but before the Colossus of Killiecrankie by the A9 road) took me back to my own misadventure with automatically flushing toilets. This escapade took place at personal computing's headwaters, the headquarters of Microsoft.

The year was 1997: Researchers publicly announced the existence of Dolly the cloned sheep, *The Simpsons* passed *The Flintstones* as the longest-running animated television series ever, and newfangled autoflush toilets were helping America stay hygienic. It was a heady time.

I was at the annual meeting of the American Association for the Advancement of Science, held that February in Seattle. Journalists attending the conference were also invited to visit Microsoft near Redmond. So I went and inevitably had to go. I left a lecture (which I recall was about the ongoing efforts to create reliable voice-recognition software, just to give you an idea of the scope of that still unsolved problem) and wandered until I found a bathroom. I entered, put the seat up, and proceeded as usual. After which, being committed to the commonweal of my fellow fellows, I tried to flush. And was thwarted at every turn.

While searching in vain for a handle or button or even dangling chain, I noticed a small, dark rectangle in the middle of which was a luminous red dot. I knew then that I was in the presence of electronic technology.

Clearly, this object was a sensor designed to automatically flush the toilet once the end user zipped away. And yet no flush would gush, no surge would purge, no swirl unfurled. I refused to leave the room before disposing of all the evidence, so I began a meticulous debugging analysis. And through a careful consideration of the geometries, relative positions, and functions of all the objects in the setup, I concluded that the sensor had been located in a place where it could be blocked by only one thing—the upraised seat. With the seat up, the system was convinced that a request was still being processed. So I put the seat down.

That simple act, the savior of millions of marriages, solved the problem. What we used to call "the electric eye" suddenly was alerted to the fact that the task was complete. Water began its flow to the sea, and another wee aliquot of processed caffeine started its journey to Puget Sound.

As I washed up, I reflected that the situation at Microsoft was probably explicable in one of two ways. One possibility was that whoever installed the componentry had used state-of-the-art motion-sensor technology along with deep ergonomic theory and application to trick men into putting down the toilet seat. The other option was that they had accidentally cobbled together a Rube Goldbergian arrangement that in effect replaced the old-fashioned toilet-seat handle with the seat itself. As a Windows user who has to click "Start" to turn my computer off, and as a man who knows that most men wouldn't try all that hard to flush in the first place, I'm betting on the latter.

SWEET AND SOILED SCIENCE

LIMBS AND HANDS FROM THE NORTHEAST TO THE SOUTHWEST

January 2007

What makes the sap run? Because he or she wants to serve in Congress. Well, that's the first answer that springs to mind this autumn day just after the November elections, and we'll get back to that subject later. But a better answer deals with a better interpretation of the question regarding maple syrup. That subject was also on my mind, I having recently returned from a trip to the Proctor Maple Research Center in Underhill Center, Vermont, while attending the annual meeting of the Society of Environmental Journalists in Burlington.

Turns out that what makes *that* sap run is devilishly complex. It's so complicated, in fact, that the only way I may ever really understand it is to have the scientists who research this question write a feature article for *Scientific American* so I can read it.

The key point, though, is that sugar maple trees have the unusual property of producing positive internal pressure after freezing and thawing. That internal pressure can tap, I mean top, that of a car tire, reaching about 40 pounds per square inch. In order to top, I mean tap, the tree, makers of maple syrup rely on the tree tap, I mean top—the branches are really where the action takes place that ultimately brings you your favorite pancake tapping. I mean topping.

Most trees have fibers filled with water, but sugar maples have air-filled fibers. "So," explains top tap (works either way) researcher Timothy Wilmot, "instead of getting the conditions you'd expect—where freezing would cause an expansion and something would come out of the tap hole when it froze—because of the physiology of the maple wood, water is actually sucked up during the freezing period. And during the thawing period, it's pushed out."

Because making the sap run—we're still talking maple trees here—requires a series of freezes and thaws, the entire industry is dependent on temperatures oscillating between a narrow range just below and just above freezing. A growing fear in the northeastern U.S. is that sustained warming will push both that temperature range and the sugar maple range north of the freezing point and border, respectively. Indeed, the sugaring season is getting shorter in Vermont but not in Canada. Yet.

By the way, I took a break in the middle of writing this story to have pancakes and Vermont maple syrup. While eating, I read a short item in the publication *Funny Times* that concerned a visit to a grade school by a firefighter. He showed the students a smoke alarm and asked if they could identify it. One kid responded, "That's how Mommy knows supper is ready." Just minutes earlier I had shut off a smoke alarm to prevent the hearing damage that ordinarily accompanies my pancake cooking.

Speaking of smoke-filled rooms, back to the election. The week before the voting, a story circulated about the practice among many politicians of using liberal—even among conservatives—dollops of those syrupy hand sanitizers when they're meeting and greeting hundreds of strangers. Seemed like a good and innocuous idea, and one of the few on which George W. Bush and Al Gore publicly agree.

But New Mexico governor Bill Richardson said he found it "condescending to the voters," according to the *New York Times*. "I'm not afraid to get my hands dirty," Richardson said. Two stats: Richardson holds the world record for most hands shaken—13,392 in eight hours at his state fair and at the University of New Mexico in 2002; a 2005 American Society for Microbiology study of more than 6,000 subjects found that 18 percent did not wash their hands after using a public restroom. So, unless New Mexicans are unusually clean or the venues had no facilities, Richardson probably shook hands with about 2,400 could-be contaminated constituents. And he may have passed along their microbes to the washed masses. Syrupticiously.

POULTRY AND POETRY

O CHICKEN NEW WORLD, THAT HAS SUCH WEIRD STUFF IN IT

August 2002

Woody Allen called one of his books *Without Feathers*, an angst-ridden response to Emily Dickinson's buoyant comment that "hope is the thing with feathers." In late May a creature seemingly brought forth from Woody's tormented subconscious was revealed to the public: the featherless chicken. Bred by a geneticist in Israel, the bird would allegedly withstand heat better—while alive, anyway. The featherless chicken thus joins the boneless chicken ("How did it walk?" Oscar Madison famously asked) and the rubber chicken as a comedy staple.

As the perpetrator of this column, I was immediately seized with gratitude, recognizing the exposed poultry for the surefire wacky-science page-filler it is. But I felt guilty taking advantage of this chicken served up on a silver platter—where's the challenge? So, having reported the existence of the undressed bird, I'm going to pass the buck and change the subject.

One of the more unpleasant tasks at *Scientific American* is to inform some people that we will not be publishing their theory/discovery/life's work. Therefore, in an attempt to flick chickens from my thoughts, I began to experiment with the pastoral Japanese haiku form as a gentler vehicle than the standard rejection letter. Here are the preliminary results of that experiment:

Your science studies
Fall from the tree like ripe fruit.
There shall we leave them.

Our greatest respect
For your research endeavors
Must remain unknown.

Feynman on bongos
Made a better argument
Than your article.

Photosynthesis
Makes oxygen from forests.
So don't waste paper.

Those examples are general, good for any occasion.
Next we have specific replies addressing some common
themes from prospective authors:

Proving Einstein wrong
Isn't all that easy, pal.
You took him lightly.

So you cloned yourself.
Please ask your new twin brother
To write the report.

Planet 10, you say?
Boy, do we have news for you.
Pluto got the ax.

We wouldn't have guessed
That your cold fusion device
Would work this badly.

Messages from Mars?
Please check your tinfoil-lined hat
We think it got wet.

You found no new gene.
A-U-G started this mess.
Toe TAG your sequence.

Though the specs look nice,
A stop sign halts your machine:
Thermo's second law.

Nice three-color map,
With adjacent states both blue.
We knew you'd need four.

Heavy hydrogen?
Congrats on your spanking-new
FBI folder.

What a waste of time
Making transgenic white mice
That contract pinkeye.

Your quantum paper
Was filled with uncertainty:
Neither here nor there.

Stop reinventing
Electromagnetism.
All's well with Maxwell.

We applaud your zeal
But they never walked abreast,
Dinosaurs and man.

No global warming?
I guess you might be correct.
But where's all the snow?

And finally:

Featherless chicken.
How does one get down off you?
Just think about it.

THE PROOF IS ON THE PAINTING

MIXING DRINKS AND CULTURE IS AN ART

May 2006

Like an examiner for the National Transportation Safety Board analyzing a plane crash, I'm trying to identify the factors that led to a recent calamity at the Milwaukee Art Museum. First, in retrospect, it's probably a bad idea to use an art museum for any kind of all-you-can-drink event.

When the event is dubbed Martini-fest—unlimited martinis for $30—the idea becomes even more questionable. Next, add a suspicious martini recipe, which included vodka and "drink mix," according to the *Milwaukee Journal Sentinel*. This situation is a classic example of experts assuming that their proficiency extends to other areas—Milwaukeeans, there's no shame in accepting your status as beer connoisseurs and consulting a specialist for the preparation of other alcoholic beverages.

In addition, the event was run by Clear Channel, the radio/billboard/concert-promoter giant, also working outside its area of expertise in an art museum. Finally, cram about 1,900 people into a space meant for about 1,400. Here's the capsule summary from the *Journal Sentinel*: "People threw up, passed out, were injured, got into altercations, and climbed onto sculptures." Which is either really bad management or a fairly banal example of postmodernism.

Fortunately, the worst-offended pieces were sturdy sculptures. But as a service to other art museums possibly planning all-you-can-drink boozefests, I got in touch with Jennifer Mass, a chemist and senior scientist at the Winterthur Museum & Country Estate in Winterthur, Delaware, to find out about the dangers that drunken revelry poses to objets d'art such as the paintings sometimes found in your better museums.

Consider the three major categories of hazardous materials. The first is ethanol, the drinkable kind of alcohol. "Paintings are typically varnished with triterpenoid resins," Mass explains. "Ethanol would be an extremely aggressive solvent for those materials. Typically what happens after museum parties where alcohol is involved—which is always a bad idea to begin with—is that you get drips that wind up on paintings. And what you see is kind of a frosted appearance to the varnish. The varnish is actually starting to dissolve."

Hors d'oeuvres also pose a danger. Imagine some indiscriminately flung meats and cheeses. "Some of the materials that we have in foods, like proteins and carbohydrates, are also used in paintings," Mass says. "And then cleaning becomes a real problem, because the same solvent that would remove the food would also remove some of the original paint."

The acid test, literally, comes when paintings encounter—how to put this delicately—an ipecascade. "You've got the low pH from the stomach acid, combined with digestive enzymes, combined with the alcohol," Mass points out. "It would be extremely damaging to an object of art. We use enzyme treatments to *clean* objects of art, so that is something that is going to be an incredibly aggressive mixture."

Ah, but if the painting needed to be cleaned anyway, might a barf bath actually be a positive? "Too many unknown materials are going to be in someone's stomach contents," Mass speculates. "You could wind up eating right through the original varnish and attacking a painting with that mixture. So I can't say that it would start the job for you." Bottom line: do not allow your priceless masterpieces to be emetically sealed.

So how close to the art should people get at museum parties that include snacks and snifters? "We tend to keep people out of the rooms where there are original objects of art when there's food and drink involved," Mass says. "What a concept. And if there are pieces that are too large to be moved, then they should be roped off." Because it's far better to be roped off than ralphed on.

SOUND PROOF

OLD SPEECH HABITS ARE ON THE LAM FOR A RESIDENT OF BUCKINGHAM

March 2001

As Professor Henry Higgins, the fictional patrician phonetician, proved in the case of Eliza Doolittle, how one speaks can be as important as what one says. Therefore, recent research involving Queen Elizabeth II must have hit like a hurricane in Hartford, Hereford, Hampshire, and the rest of the scepter'd isle: the queen no longer speaks the Queen's English. Well, not the Queen's English of half a century ago, anyway.

The changing nature of the queen's pronunciations was investigated by members of the Macquarie Center for Cognitive Science and the Speech Hearing and Language Research Center of Macquarie University. (Those institutions are in Australia, where some residents speak the Queensland English.) The researchers, who published the study in *Nature*, analyzed the vowel sounds made by the queen in Christmas messages from the 1950s and the 1980s. The authors note that they received permission from Buckingham Palace to perform the research, which proves that the Beatles were right and then wrong when they said, "Her Majesty's a pretty nice girl, but she doesn't have a lot to say."

Also scrutinized was the so-called standard southern British (SSB) accent, more likely to come from the mouths of the young and middle class. The researchers looked to 1980s recordings of female announcers on the BBC to compare the SSB to QE II. The inescapable conclusion: from the 1950s to the 1980s, the queen did indeed move her vowels. Although she still sounds distinct from the commoners on television and radio, the queen's accent by the 1980s was closer to regular folk than it had been three decades previous. Which proves that the Beatles were right and then right again when they continued, "Her Majesty's a pretty nice girl, but she changes from day to day."

The subtle move toward more common-denominator vocalizations may be the price of doing business in societies less and less dominated by adherence to traditional social castes. I am often reminded of the importance of similar speech patterns in engendering a sense of community. In my own Bronx neighborhood, for example, visitors can expect to be ritually greeted upon entering any of the local dining establishments with the welcoming words, "Youse wanna cuppuh cawfee?" The correct response to this query is, "Shaw, tanks." The incorrect response, "Why, yes, a splash of your most mellow Arabican would indeed be in order," can arouse suspicious glances that may in the fullness of time lead to beatings upon the capacious upside of one's head.

My example, of course, involves both pronunciation and the separate issue of actual word usage. The choice of words is also an important indicator of one's relationship with the rest of society. Keith Greiner took this idea to heart recently when he broke down every single presidential inaugural address and counted the number of self-related words, such as *I, me, my,* and *mine*, as well as inclusive words, like *we, us, our,* and *ours.*

Greiner, who deals professionally with higher education data for an Iowa state agency, did the study to satisfy his personal curiosity and because the winters are very long in Iowa. He found that "since James Garfield's address in 1881, the percentage of words describing the inclusive 'we' relationship has grown dramatically." According to a Greiner graph, inclusive words account for about 2 percent of most speeches before Garfield but rise thereafter to an average of approximately 6 percent and hit a high of 10 percent for Ronald Reagan a century later.

Restricting the study to inaugural addresses successfully avoided potential confusion concerning presidential utterances that sound like we. These include the Francophone Thomas Jefferson's *"oui,"* the diminutive James Madison's self-deprecating self-description, "wee," and the rotund William Howard Taft's jubilant exclamation upon successfully extricating himself from the White House bathtub, "Weeeee."

So the queen sounds more like everyone else, and our presidents talk more like they *are* everyone else. Of course, the queen's speech no doubt changed naturally over time. Presidential communications alterations, on the other hand, may in part be conscious and manipulative, an attempt to appear in tune with the masses. Another wee thing to consider for us da people.

THINKING OUTSIDE THE BOX

August 1999

Who knew? Turns out that some six million General Motors cars have been traversing the highways and byways of America this decade while carrying hidden black boxes, stripped-down versions of the flight-data recorders that sometimes reveal the causes of airline catastrophes. The latest version of the recorder, known as a sensing and diagnostic module (SDM), keeps track of the last five seconds before an impact. It catalogs speed, the position of the gas pedal, when the brakes were finally applied and whether the driver was belted, all in an attempt to improve safety through research.

Unfortunately, the fundamental flaw in the automobile black box business remains the quality of the available information. The skeletal data about the car leave virtually untold the story of the weak link: the driver. A truly valuable system might be able to give detailed data about the man or woman, or pet, behind the wheel. For example:

Case I. Lysergically enhanced Deadhead driving original Volkswagen Beetle down San Francisco's Lombard Street thinks he sees Jerry (Garcia). Makes beeline for same. Destroys $76,000 worth of floral arrangements.

Case II. Woman in Scottsdale, Ariz., driving Mercury Marquis has parakeet perched on middle finger of left hand, mirror between thumb and forefinger of left hand for parakeet to observe self. Cigarette in right hand burning down. Attempt made with right hand to manipulate fresh cigarette into position to be ignited by currently lit cigarette. Artificial knees provide insufficient steering proficiency.

Case III. New York City cab driver uses both hands to flip off second cab driver, who hails from neighboring country of origin.

Case IV. Cornell University student skids down entire length of ice-covered State Street with both feet jammed on brake pedal, comes to stop in snowdrift on the Commons.

Case V. Left engine flameout on final approach to LAX. Wrong data recorder.

Case VI. Little old man in Boca Raton, Fla., driving black Lincoln Continental at 2 mph in Publix parking lot thinks he sees Jerry (Seinfeld), signals left, goes right. Second little old man trailing first little old man, also driving black Lincoln Continental, veers to right at 4 mph in attempt to pass first little old man while still in presumed left turn. Ensuing fender-bender sets off 23-car pileup within parking lot. Vehicle damage limited to scratches, but paramedics treat 14 drivers for palpitations.

Case VII. Illinois man driving used police car tries to jump open drawbridge over Chicago River.

Cutting to the car chase, good data concerning what drivers were up to just before totaling on the turnpike are hard to come by: not everyone will admit to their dopey stunts just before impact, and investigators can only do so much in reconstructing a driver's multitasking.

Quality data may appear soon, however. The National Highway Traffic Safety Administration is currently experimenting with an unobtrusive onboard camera system designed to get good looks at the kinds of things drivers do in addition to driving.

The bet here, if people truly forget that they are being watched, is that the record will show drivers conspiring in their own misery via brewskies, lead foots, mascara, cassettes, cellular telephones, doggies, children, cigarette lighters, sexual activity and trying to use the wipers to move one of those annoying leaflets, placed on your windshield while you were busy shopping, into position to be snatched off with your left hand as you're driving. Because, as usual, the infinite variety of questionable human behavior remains the ultimate black box.

NAME RECOGNITION

WHAT'S IN A NAME? WOULD MY AUNT ROSE HAVE BEEN AS SWEET HAD SHE BEEN MY AUNT PETUNIA?

September 2000

Tiger, Tiger, golfing keen
From the teebox to the green
Would you be the litter's pick
By your real name, young Eldrick?
(with apologies to William Blake)

A city full of people forced to attract one another's attention with an endless chorus of "Yo!" would be a ponderous place, or at least sound suspiciously like New York City. Therefore, handles come in handy. Theoretically, a name is merely a designation, a way to distinguish one individual from another. But various studies over the years have shown that some names also carry the weight of expectations. And those expectations, primarily on the parts of the parents who dubbed little Dub, can subtly influence the dubbee.

James Bruning has studied the appellation issue for some three decades, as a psychologist at Ohio University. (His institution's name often gets it confused with that other school that has all the big-name running backs, who, coincidentally, have their names on their backs when they run.) Bruning's years of research lead him to offer this counsel for couples musing on names for the new arrival: the baby will be an adult for most of its life. "I always advise parents to at least put a Mr. or Mrs., or President, or King or Queen—some title that says 'adult'—in front of the name," he says. "Do that, and I think you very quickly could drop a lot of choices." If nothing else, we could avoid a future where the nursing homes are teeming with Briannas, Kaitlyns, Austins, and Tylers.

Bruning's most recent foray into the name game, published in the latest issue of the *Journal of Social Psychology*, looked at how people's prejudices about names might lead to presumptions about someone's chances for career success. Twenty students who served as study subjects knew only two things about hypothetical jobseekers: their first names and the work they were interested in. The sixteen names and sixteen jobs, however, had been carefully chosen to enable the consideration of three criteria.

The first was simply whether the name was male or female. Hank and Francis, for example, are men, and Emma and Hester are women.

The second variable was the perceived masculinity or femininity of the name, based on the results of a large survey. Hank was not only a guy name but was also judged to be a strapping, meat-eating-type guy name. On the other hand, Francis was rated among the most feminine of men's names. (Francis Albert in combination, however, was no doubt a very masculine man's moniker, at least while Sinatra was alive and moody. Nevertheless, honesty being the best policy, Francis knew he was better off being Frank.) Emma was one of the study's feminine female names, whereas Hester was thought to be a masculine female name. (Hey, Hawthorne stitched the scarlet letter on a Hester, not a Susie.)

The final consideration was the stereotypical masculine or feminine nature of the job. Most people assume, for example, that a plumber or truck driver is going to be a man and that a manicurist or flight attendant is a woman. They apparently haven't flown lately, but that's what they assume.

The data from the twenty Dicks and Janes showed, no surprise, that they put their money most confidently on women with feminine names trying for "female" jobs and on men with manly names trying for "male" jobs. "I wouldn't overestimate the impact of names," Bruning warns, "but at the same time, names are an important part of first impressions." And a first impression can be a lasting one. If you had to open one of two doors, to reveal an athlete for you to market worldwide, who would you hope came out: the Eldrick or the Tiger?

CHARMED, I'M SURE

FOR THE SCIENTIFICALLY BRIGHT BUT SOCIALLY BEFUDDLED, A DAY OF ETIQUETTE INSTRUCTION MIGHT BE JUST WHAT THE PH.D. ORDERED

April 2001

It's a classic problem for the average scientist-in-training: Do you pick your teeth with your acceptance letter from the Massachusetts Institute of Technology or with the envelope it came in? (The correct answer is neither: you use the paper clip holding together your orientation materials.)

But seriously, for a moment anyway, M.I.T. recognized the fact that it was sending some students out into the world who were apparently more comfortable crossing a Wheatstone bridge than crossing to the other side of a room to introduce themselves. They were more at ease asking for a Dewar flask than asking, "Do you want to dance?" They could insert a gene better than they could insert themselves into a conversation. Before I search for a geology reference, you get the idea. So in early February 2001,

M.I.T. invited any and all students to voluntarily attend its eighth annual charm school.

"We used to refer to it as 'Degeekifying M.I.T.,'" says Katherine O'Dair, charm school coordinator and assistant dean for student life programs. "But we got rid of any references to geeks. No one wants to be thought of that way." (So, O'Dair must have been thrilled with the *New York Times*. The headline of its charm school coverage included the phrase "Geeks at M.I.T.") It's not clear how many students showed up thinking it was a symposium on quarks, but about 800 did wind up attending—about 8 percent of the student body.

I was particularly interested in the M.I.T. event because of psychic etiquette wounds I experienced in my own scientific education. At the institution where I attended graduate school, the chemistry department rewarded the students with a weekly treat. Every Wednesday at 4:30 P.M. a big bag of bagels was delivered to the student lounge in an exercise that became known as "bagel minute." Not since buzz bombs rained down on London have people raced to a common destination with a greater sense of urgency. Bagel minute was nasty, brutish, and short. If you showed up at 4:31, all that was left were some stray schmears of cream cheese and the guilty faces of the survivors.

M.I.T.'s charm school attempts, in a day, to at least expose students to the many guidelines of behavior that will help them move gracefully into the polite society that their postgraduate lives should include. Classes in table manners

will most likely do away with any bagel-minute-like es-
capades. Dress-for-success instruction will come in particularly handy for the young man who showed up wearing a
cap on which was written, simply, "PIMP."

Students were also free to sit at the feet of experts in
both business and cell phone etiquette. Unfortunately,
many more seemed interested in the former than the latter, a situation that needs quick remedy if my train trip
from New York City was any indication: half a dozen loud
cell phone conversations took place in my car all the way to
Boston.

Perhaps the highlight of M.I.T.'s charm school was the
half-hour class on flirting, which ran repeatedly during the
day. (One might think that teaching college kids how to flirt
would be as necessary as teaching a nightingale to sing,
but one might be wrong.) In each session, the mentors separated the men from the women and asked members in
each group how they could tell if someone they had just
met at a party liked them. The top two reasons the men
thought a woman might be interested was that she made
eye contact and seemed genuinely engaged in the conversation. The top two reasons the women thought a man
might be into them was that "they stare at me and they
turn red." And so I was reminded that our tree-swinging
origins still beckon. Which is all the more reason for learning how to flawlessly finger the fondue fork.

UP THE LAZY CREEK

THE MORE THINGS CHANGE,
THE MORE THEY'RE NOT THE SAME

June 2006

I turned this column in very late. I just couldn't get started writing it. Low energy. You know how it is.

Fortunately, my editor can take no action against me, because my lateness, I was delighted to discover, was in fact brought about by a disease: I clearly suffer from "motivational deficiency disorder." The *British Medical Journal*, the praises of which were sung in this space in March 2006 [See Annual Rapport, page 86], reported on this novel malaise in its April 1 issue. "Extreme laziness," the *BMJ* piece explains, "may have a medical basis, says a group of high-profile Australian scientists, describing a new condition called motivational deficiency disorder (MoDeD)." (MoDeD is most definitely not to be confused with Mos Def, who is clearly not a sufferer of MoDeD.)

The article went on to quote a Dr. Leth Argos as one of the discoverers of the disorder. The allusion to lethargy should have been the tip-off, even if you missed the date, that the article was an April Fools' joke. The MoDeD giveaway was the citing of a drug called Strivor, which was allegedly so successful in treating the disease that "one young man who could not leave his sofa is now working as an investment adviser." Talk about your dangerous side effects.

The prank, however, had a purpose: the piece was designed to bring attention to a conference on so-called disease mongering, the medicalization of ordinary conditions, which thereby opens markets for drugs to treat them as illnesses. The stunt, however, may have inadvertently demonstrated the existence of a true ailment. Because a quick search of the Internet reveals that numerous news outlets picked up the *BMJ* press release and ran it without a hint of skepticism. That's just motivationally deficient journalism.

In other factual news, hurricane season is here again, accompanied by reminders of the threat of terrorism so constant that the fear of a terrorist attack is probably itself a new malady. (Even though it's still heart disease, cancer, or some driver on a bender or a cell phone that's probably going to get you.) But the obvious and dire need to be ready for emergencies notwithstanding, seven candidates for top jobs, including the directorship of the Federal Emergency Management Agency (FEMA), told the *New York Times* that they had removed themselves from consideration because they weren't sure the Bush administration was really serious about emergency management. (The acting director of FEMA, R. David Paulison, was eventually nominated for that top job.)

I bring this up only because Representative Harold Rogers of Kentucky, chair of the House subcommittee that controls the purse strings of the Department of Homeland Security and thus of FEMA, actually said, "Let the word go forth from this place that we want a permanent director of FEMA, and we want these regional directors and division directors to stop acting and be permanent. Because I want somebody responsible that we can turn to."

Rogers's use of the phrase "let the word go forth from this place" conjured up memories of another statement that began almost the same way. In his inaugural address, President John F. Kennedy said, "Let the word go forth from this time and place, to friend and foe alike, that the torch has been passed to a new generation of Americans—born in this century, tempered by war, disciplined by a hard and bitter peace, proud of our ancient heritage, and unwilling to witness or permit the slow undoing of those human rights to which this nation has always been committed, and to which we are committed today at home and around the world." In forty-five years, "let the word go forth" has gone from introducing a sweeping summation of who we are and what we stand for to announcing frustration over the inability to find someone to run FEMA. Talk about motivational deficiency.

EINSTEIN'S PARROT

A GREAT BRAIN AND A BIRD BRAIN
SPEND TIME TOGETHER

July 2004

In late April 2004 the Associated Press reported the discovery of a diary written by a woman, Johanna Fantova, who was a close friend of Albert Einstein. "The sixty-two-page diary, written in German, was discovered in February in Fantova's files at Princeton University's Firestone Library, where she had worked as a curator," the AP story noted. One fascinating revelation of the diary is that Einstein received a parrot as a seventy-fifth-birthday gift. According to the AP, "After deciding the bird was depressed, Einstein tried to alter its mood by telling bad jokes."

Parrots can live for a century. In early May I may (or may not) have encountered a parrot that may (or may not) have been the bird entertained by Einstein. Speaking in German-accented English, the parrot recited a monologue. What follows is a transcript of that monologue:

> "How do I order beer in a bar? I say 'Ein stein for Einstein.' Hey, Parrot, what's the difference between a wild boar and Niels Bohr? When I say that God doesn't play dice, a wild boar doesn't tell me to stop telling God what to do. I hate that. So what do you say to the man who developed the exclusion principle? You say, 'Pauli want a cracker?' Wolfgang Pauli, get it? Hello, is this thing on? Testing, one, two. Hey, Parrot, I had a dream where I made love to Rita Hayworth for an hour. Well, for her it was an hour. For me, thirty-five seconds. That's relativity. Okay, Newton is standing on the shoulders of a giant, and he says, 'Giant, how do I get down off you?' and the giant says, 'You don't get down off me, you get down off a duck.' I love that one. Parrot, tell me, what is a Lorentz contraction? That's when Mrs. Lorentz knows the baby is coming. It's a timed dilation, not a time dilation, get it? Let's see, two guys walk into an h-bar. An H-BAR. If you knew any physics you'd be on the floor, I swear. Uh, if Ruby Keeler married, uh, John Wheeler, became a doctor and got a job in Vegas, she'd be Ruby Keeler Wheeler the healer dealer. So what would people

say if Paul Dirac fell on Jane Russell? They'd say, 'Look at Dirac on Jane Russell.' Oh, they'd say it, trust me. Okay, there are these twins, see. They're twenty years old. And one of them goes zipping around the universe really fast while the other one stays on Earth. The twin who was zipping around comes back, and he's maybe a year older, and he goes to find his brother. And the brother is now ninety-five years old. And the young twin comes up to him. The old twin looks at the young twin, and tears come to his eyes. And the young twin says, 'Why are you crying?' And the old twin says, 'I'm so happy.' And the young twin says, 'To see me?' And the old twin, he says, 'Yes. The $100 you owed me when you left. It's now $100,000.' From the compounding interest. Oy, these are the jokes, Parrot. What, you don't like living in a cage? Yeah, try being the most famous man in the world. I can't even go out for a haircut. You know, you're a good listener for a parrot. Oh boy, it looks like you just did a Brownian movement. Good thing I lined the cage with my cosmological constant proposal. That proposal was my second biggest mistake. My biggest mistake was my proposal to my first wife. Ba-dum-bum. Parrot, if you had a plastic deer on your lawn covered in Christmas lights, turning them on would give you the faux doe electric effect. Whaddya call it when Leo Szilard and Enrico Fermi pull up an anchor? A chain retraction! Not so good? You should hear me play the violin. So Schrödinger and Heisenberg are driving down the road, and Heisenberg says, 'Hey, I think you just ran over a cat.' And Schrödinger, he says, 'Is it dead?' And Heisenberg says, heh heh, get this: 'I can't be certain.' Okay, so the smartest man in the world is talking to a parrot. Hey, Parrot, that's not a joke, that's my life."

DIVINING COMEDY

CAN RESEARCHERS DISSECT HUMOR WITHOUT KILLING THE PATIENCE?

March 2002

Last September, the British Association for the Advancement of Science (BAAS) announced a plan to discover the world's funniest joke. This quest for the joke of all jokes, the wisest of cracks, the topper de tutti toppi, was to be conducted using a double-pronged approach in which visitors to a Website could submit jokes and vote on those already available for judgment. According to the journal *Nature*, visitors to the site (www.laughlab.co.uk) were asked to fill out a brief questionnaire "about their age, gender, and nationality, as well as a brief cognition quiz." The associations between jokes and survey responses would theoretically make possible "the largest-ever look at the psychology of humor."

As the writer of what passes for a humor column (which at *Scientific American* is like making the best Sloppy Joes at the culinary institute), I naturally took an interest. My initial reaction was summed up by taking advantage of certain principles of fluid dynamics to produce what is known as a Bronx cheer, or, in England, a raspberry. I felt this way because jokes tend to be on the low end of the funnymeter. (The accent is on the second, not first, syllable.) Confirming my prejudice, last December the BAAS sheepishly announced the Laugh Lab's winning entry, the funniest joke in the world, according to science:

> Sherlock Holmes and Dr. Watson are going camping. They pitch their tent under the stars and go to sleep. Sometime in the middle of the night Holmes wakes Watson up.

I have to interrupt the joke already to talk about the Reuters news service coverage of this research. *Their* version of the joke opens with, "Famed fictional detective Sherlock Holmes and his gruff assistant Dr. Watson ..." (Neil Simon just called, weeping.) I mean, if you're telling the world's funniest joke to someone who doesn't know who Holmes and Watson are, you're like the guy at the aforementioned culinary institute who was just wasting thyme.

Anyway, let us return to the yuckfest. Holmes and Watson are camping. It is dark. We begin:

> HOLMES: Watson, look up at the stars, and tell me what you deduce.
> WATSON: I see millions of stars, and if there are millions of stars, and if even a few of those have planets, it is quite likely that there are some planets like Earth, and if there are a few planets like Earth out there, there might also be life.

HOLMES: Watson, you idiot, somebody stole our tent!

It's really not an awful joke, especially when you tell it right, which means that you probably don't mention the tent until the punch line, and Holmes just says to look up, not to look up at the stars. Then the listener gets to make all the connections, for an even more delectable aesthetic guffawing experience. (How do I know so much about comedy, you wonder? Easy. I watch a lot of television. Especially the Sunday-morning political roundtables.)

Laugh Lab researchers, whom I rib in the spirit of good humor, might benefit from a reading of Robert R. Provine's book *Laughter: A Scientific Investigation*. Or better yet, they can read Frans B. M. De Waal's review of it in the December 2000 issue of *Scientific American*, as I did. (The mark of the true faux intellectual is to read reviews rather than the actual books, allowing one to comment as if one really knew anything. The faux intellectual also uses words like "faux.")

De Waal notes, "One of the revelations of this book is that the stand-up comedy model of laughter as a response to jokes is mistaken. The large majority of laughs measured by Provine and his students . . . occurred after statements that were far from humorous," which reveals that social relationships are probably the biggest key to humor. You can tell a joke, but you can't really "tell" Kramer exploding into Jerry's apartment, or Norton addressing the golf ball, or the funeral of Chuckles the Clown. As Heisenberg did not say to the electron, "You just had to be there."

NAMING NAMES

MUCH ADO ABOUT N

November 2005

There had actually been some good news for a change, for a while. The ivory-billed woodpecker, long thought to be extinct, turned out not to be. As a bird-watcher who thrills to any fleeting glimpse of a plain old pileated woodpecker, not to mention the redbellies, hairies, and downies that commonly slam their heads into trees in my own Bronx backyard, I imagined how great it would be to see an ivory bill. And then I imagined that it's probably in the best long-term survival interests of any species to keep the word "ivory" out of its name. I therefore mused that the ivory-billed woodpecker should henceforth be known as the cheap-Formica-billed woodpecker. You know, for its own good.

Those happy thoughts disappeared along with New Orleans. Like most of the civilized world, I went from sad to stunned to seething as the city was swamped, just days ago as I write. Then I heard a highly respected journalist make a small mistake on national television. And, in direct contrast to the agencies that deal with disasters, I probably overreacted. Because I went berserk: full-out John-McEnroe-bad-line-call insane. Temporarily, I hope. Here's what happened.

The October 2001 issue of *Scientific American* featured a depressingly prescient article by contributing editor Mark Fischetti entitled "Drowning New Orleans." The piece reads as if Fischetti wrote it in the days following Hurricane Katrina's assault on the city, describing in detail almost exactly the scenario that engulfed the gulf—and what could have been done to prevent it. Fischetti thus became a frequent guest on television news programs in the early days of September.

One such TV appearance came on Sunday, September 4, 2005 (a date which will live inflaming me), on *Meet the Press*. NBC News Washington bureau chief and *Meet the Press* moderator Tim Russert introduced Fischetti and noted that his article had appeared in—buckle up—*Scientific America*. (The written transcript of the program corrects the error, but it's clear in the audio available through the NBC Website.)

This mistake is common. I've lost count of the number of people I've met who say, "Oh, I read *Scientific America* all the time." To which I say to myself, "No, you don't."

So why did I get so mad this time? There were certainly much more pressing issues that day than the correct name of this publication. Russert's mistake might have been a mere tongue slip. But I'm betting that the more likely explanation for the name truncation is that most muckety-mucks, whether in politics or journalism, are unfamiliar with *Scientific American* because they don't pay all that much attention to science in general. Which is ironic, because Fischetti's piece isn't the only one in these pages that can tell the reader what will be happening years down the road, whereas most news outlets only tell you what happened yesterday.

Actually, *Moot the Press* and I have had issues for some time. Back in the dark days before the turn of the millennium, Y2K was an alleged impending crisis. The renowned computer scientist, systems analyst, and cultural anthropologist Pat Robertson appeared with Russert to explain that the coming computer meltdown was going to cripple us. (Yes, this is the same Pat Robertson who recently pulpitized in favor of assassinating the duly elected president of a sovereign nation, then denied it and then apologized for it.) I wrote a letter to the producer suggesting that a serious discussion of the Y2K issue would require guests with greater expertise in the field than a televangelist has.

So it is definitely a positive development that people like Mark Fischetti, people who actually know stuff, get invited to appear on national news programs, along with spinning politicians. Having some scientists on would also be good. And it would be nice if you got our name right. Because it's inconceivable that a national news host could refer to *The Wall Street Journey, Newswake,* or *Tim,* Tim.

NOTES FROM THE UNDERGROUND

December 1999

Neither rain, nor sleet, nor gloom of night will stop readers from sending mail. "Antigravity" gets its fair share. Regular readers recognize it as a somewhat offbeat take on science, a break from the rest of the magazine's exposition of the weighty work, the gravitas, of teasing out nature's secrets.

Some of the mail decries the very existence of this column, with the reader feeling cheated out of two-thirds of a page of meat and potatoes. To them, I offer only regrets that they care not for the occasional ice cream cone and advice that they turn the page with a greater sense of urgency.

Some mail carries the reader's umbrage with me. To them, I offer thanks for sharing their thoughts and advice that they get their own magazine column. (And this note: Letters containing the phrase "I have a sense of humor, but ..." inevitably announce the lack of same.) Amazingly, some mail indicates that the reader actually likes the column, proving that there's no accounting for taste.

Finally, some mail educates. In September 1999 [see Strife After Death, page 22], this space discussed the matter of dead rattlesnakes still capable of delivering nasty bites. This entry prompted a response from Thomas Reisner of the literature department at Laval University in Quebec: "[The] review of a warning recently published in the *New England Journal of Medicine*, concerning the hazards of manipulating dead rattlesnakes prematurely, rang a bell with me. On further reflection, I recalled having come across the idea of snakes inflicting bites on their handlers postmortem in, of all places, the poetical works of Percy B. Shelley.

"In 1820, when Shelley showed his recently completed *Witch of Atlas* to his wife Mary (of Frankenstein fame), she was apparently unimpressed. Her response goaded him into writing a good-natured apology for the poem, beginning with the lines:

> How, my dear Mary,—are you critic-bitten
> (For vipers kill, though dead) by some review,
> That you condemn these verses I have written,
> Because they tell no story, false or true?
> What, though no mice are caught by a young kitten,
> May it not leap and play as grown cats do,

Till its claws come? Prithee, for this one time,
Content thee with a visionary rhyme.

"Since at the time the Shelleys were living near Pisa, in northern Italy (a region infested with vipers, though not with rattlesnakes), his allusion may have been based on personal experience. In any event, there is, I believe, something deeply satisfying in seeing the findings of modern science scooped by a mere Romantic, almost two centuries earlier!"

There is also something deeply satisfying in, even for a moment, bridging the gap between C. P. Snow's two cultures. Especially in light of another recent letter to the *New England Journal of Medicine*, from Howard Fischer of Children's Hospital of Michigan. He recounts the sad story of a hospitalized fifty-one-year-old high school teacher. This fellow, imprisoned by the various tubes and lines attached to him, remarked that he felt as though he were in "Peter Coffin's inn." This reference to the claustrophobic lodging house in *Moby Dick* was lost on a nurse, who heard the word "coffin," put two and two together to make twenty-two and assumed the teacher might be suicidal. The patient then had to prove himself to the psychiatrists who were brought in to make sure he wasn't planning the mortal coil shuffle. (The nurse might think this odd maneuver refers to a dance step.) Fischer notes that "physicians and nurses need a broader education in the humanities."

Indeed, even in the sciences we should all strive to be men and women of letters. Or at least postcards.

FINAL FRONTIER EXAM

HERE'S ONE WAY TO FIND OUT IF YOU HAVE AT LEAST A LITTLE BIT OF THE RIGHT STUFF.

December 2000

A company with ties to NASA, Dreamtime Holdings Inc., proposed—at meetings Monday with CBS, ABC, and Fox—a show that would use NASA facilities at the Johnson Space Center in Houston to train twenty contestants hoping to be selected to spend a week aboard the new International Space Station, executives at the three networks said.

—*New York Times*, Sept. 21, 2000

Thank you for your interest in being a contestant on Space Survivor (working title). Because of the great interest on the part of the public, we have received literally thousands of applications. In order to limit our interviews to those individuals most knowledgeable about space, we have created the following series of multiple-choice questions. Please take no more than five minutes to answer the following. Good luck, live long and prosper, use a No. 2 pencil.

Questionnaire for prospective contestants on *Space Survivor* (working title):

The shuttle is

a) the U.S. spacecraft that lands like an airplane and is eventually launched back into orbit

b) still circling somewhere between Logan and LaGuardia

MACHOs are

a) what astronomers call "massive compact halo objects"

b) one of the gangs in *West Side Story*

Retrograde motion is

a) the apparent reversal of a planet's orbit resulting from the relative position of that planet and Earth

b) when you get left back in school

The Inflationary Universe refers to

a) a model in which the universe went through a brief but huge expansion

b) the store where Marlon Brando buys pants

A Pulsar is

a) a rapidly rotating neutron star sending out pulses of electromagnetic radiation

b) a prize for outstanding journalistic achievement

A Galaxy is

a) a large group of stars and associated matter

b) probably up on blocks in the front yard

The three-degree microwave background radiation is

a) the nearly isotropic energy remnant of the big bang

b) gonna take forever to bake your potato

A countdown is

a) the elapsed time leading to a lift-off

b) when they finally drive the stake into Dracula

The Apollo missions were

a) the efforts to send teams of three astronauts to the moon

b) the plots of *Rocky* and *Rocky II*

The Red Planet refers to

a) Mars

b) Clark Kent's socialist newspaper

A supernova is

a) the explosion of a star

b) a really good episode of that PBS show

"Houston, we've had a problem" are the famous words uttered by

a) Jim Lovell, commander of the crippled *Apollo 13* spacecraft

b) Bobby Brown

White dwarfs are

a) hot core remnants of burned-out stars of roughly the same mass as our sun

b) the last Knicks off the bench

Charon is

a) the moon of Pluto

b) when you give half your peanut butter sandwich
to a friend

The Vomit Comet is

a) the airplane that briefly approximates weightless
conditions, used in astronaut training
b) the worst nickname ever for an Olympic sprinter

John Glenn is

a) the first American to orbit Earth, the oldest man
ever in space, a former U.S. senator from Ohio,
a former Marine pilot
b) pretty ticked off if he's read this far

Cosmology is

a) the science of the origin and structure of the universe
b) the science of Helen Gurley Brown

The Keck is

a) the Hawaiian observatory featuring twin telescopes
that enable astronomers to probe the deepest regions
of the universe
b) wide right by Norwood: Giants 20, Bills 19,
Super Bowl XXV

Buzz Aldrin was

a) the second man on the moon
b) what the other test pilots used to do to Aldrin

An asteroid is

a) a planetary body usually between the orbits of
Mars and Jupiter, with a diameter of less than 500 miles
b) no excuse for missing work

Extra-credit question:

Daniel S. Goldin is

a) the administrator of NASA
b) going to take one small step off a high building
before he takes the one giant leap of sending a
game-show contestant into space

Acknowledgments

On Yogi Berra Appreciation Day in 1947, the catcher commented, "I want to thank you for making this day necessary." So I'd like to thank some people for making this book necessary. Thanks to my family and friends for behaviors worth noting and on occasion writing about, as well as for putting me onto stories they think might have column potential. Fran Newburg at *Scientific American* has dealt with the logistics of turning the columns into a volume. My great friend John Rennie, the magazine's editor-in-chief, often supplies suggestions or even donates lines to the columns. The column space would not exist were it not for Marguerite Holloway, former news editor at *Scientific American*. So blame her. Phil Yam, her successor, made time while editing the magazine's entire news section to be my editor as well. Special thanks to my current editor, Molly Frances, who always makes the columns better than what I originally wrote. And thanks to the readers of *Scientific American* magazine, without whose patronage there never would have been enough "Anti Gravity" columns for this collection.

Index